Praise for *Bringing Intuition to Work*

"*Bringing Intuition to Work* illuminates the power, benefit, and truth of our intuitive nature."
—Martin Rutte, Co-Author of *Chicken Soup for the Soul at Work*

"I work with people who are affected by stress originating in the workplace. The practical yet sensitive approach found in *Bringing Intuition to Work* offers a powerful method for taking control of one's life both at work and home. Gina's step-by-step approach makes some very difficult and abstract concepts understandable to everyone, and will benefit many people."

—Stanley Yantis, Psychiatrist

"*Bringing Intuition to Work* offers quick, easy-to-understand techniques that fit quite nicely into a busy workday. The tools have greatly helped me in my work with clients and in my personal life as well. I recommend this book to people in any career field."

—Maureen Belle, Environmental Designer; Lecturer; and
Author of *Gaiamancy: Creating Harmonious Environments*

BRINGING INTUITION TO WORK

BRINGING INTUITION TO WORK

A Quick Step-by-Step Approach

Gina Giacomini

INNERVISIONS
PUBLICATIONS

Coloma, California

Published by: **Innervisions Publications**
P. O. Box 213
Coloma, CA 95613

Editors: Ellen Kleiner, Chris Monroe, Susan Borquez-Dougherty,
Tony and Janeen Clark, Jim Westfall
Book design and production: James Marquez
Illustrations: Rick Meadows, Magda Moss
Cover design and production: Josh Byrd, Joe David Designs, Skye Kauffman,
Magda Moss, Mark Leder Adams
Front cover photograph: Steve Armantrout
Internet research: Gia Estrada

Printed in the United States of America on acid-free recycled paper

Publisher's Cataloging-in-Publication Data
Giacomini, Gina
Bringing intuition to work : a quick step-by step approach
/ by Gina Giacomini — 1st ed.
p. cm.
LCCN: 99-94222
ISBN: 0-9669427-0-1

1. Intuition (Psychology). 2. Success in business. 3. Performance.
4. Self-realization. I. Title.

BF315.5.G53 1999   153.4'4
                          QB199-898

10 9 8 7 6 5 4 3 2 1

With special thanks to:

My brother Jon, whose passing made me look within
Mom and Dad, sisters, brothers, family and friends, for their all-around
    support and belief in me throughout this writing process
My sister Toni, for always being there for me
My sister Sue, for the her encouragement and for being a second mom
Chris, John, and the Monroes—I couldn't ask for better friends and family
Jeannie, for the friendship, help, and support beyond what most could
    manage or even understand
Jim, for the moral support, friendship, plane rides, and evening walks with
    Hotdog, Buddy, and Raven Maniac
Janeen and Tony, for their help, patience, and friendship
Maureen, for gently guiding and showing me which potholes to avoid along
    the way
Susie and Buddy, for their ideas and sarcasm when I needed them most
Josh, for all your help into the late nights with smoothies in hand—without
    you this book would not have happened
James, whose patience, expertise, and support were instrumental throughout
    this journey
The Earthtrek gang—thanks for the water fights, food fights, bowling
    nights, and fun on and off the river
My Charter Community School family, whose love and support made this
    book possible
Vicki, for her enthusiasm, ideas, and friendship along the way
Ellen Kleiner, for all the support and help on my first literary venture
David Christian-Hamblin, for the advice and help
Hats off to the Liver River Group—you boys were so much fun and helped
    me cut loose in the last stages of my book
My homeschool families and students, who patiently listened and shared in
    this process
Rick, who isn't quite sure what he's gotten himself into, and has been a
    wonderful surprise
Midori, for the great massages and conversations

This book is dedicated to my children,
Tyler and Courtney,
who taught me what it is to love
and who bring me such happiness and joy.

A special dedication to two wonderful human beings
and fellow river guides, Raymond Caudwell and Andy Lee:
Your spirit and love of life will live on with those of us
who were enriched by knowing you.

Contents

Introduction

Often you just have to rely on your intuition.
— Bill Gates

Life is more intricate, chaotic, and illusional than any ride we could possibly imagine, even in our wildest dreams. It can bring the greatest joy, the deepest hurt, the ultimate excitement, and the darkest suicidal depression. Just when we think we can make some sense of it, life changes, and the makeshift tools we used to cope in the past seem out of date and useless. For more enduring coping strategies, we simply need to look within and view the world through new eyes, using our inner awareness and intuition.

Awareness is the ability to recognize, understand, and transform what is happening around us. Intuition is the faculty for attaining direct knowledge without relying on rational thought. We all know we use our five outer senses throughout the workday. What we may not know is that we are also using our inner senses.

Now is the time to start using inner as well as outer senses consciously, integrating them into your day. This integration will allow intuition to become part of your daily life, which in turn will enhance your abilities and optimize your performance at work.

This book is designed to help you connect with your inner awareness and unite with your intuition. I have been teaching inner awareness to individuals, groups, and businesses for the past twelve years and decided to write this book at the request of various clients who have attended my seminars. It is essentially a comprehensive manual of exercises I developed and also shares some insights I discovered while teaching. All the exercises in the book are based on simple principles. Some of the information was graciously taught to me, parts came as flashes of inspiration, other parts were discovered while working with people's energy, and the rest was forged though adversity. ~Chapter 1 describes ways of expanding personal awareness so you can walk through a busy workday using a more subtle yet more powerful approach. ~Chapter 2 points the way to the calm center within, where it is possible to separate from chaos long enough to find the clarity needed to cope. ~Chapter 3 shows how to use intention to set daily personal goals. ~Chapter 4 provides techniques for working within life's flow to meet deadlines instead of pushing through each day's agenda. ~Chapter 5 shows how to utilize a neutral energy source rather than deplete the physical body's limited energy reserves. ~Chapter 6 offers tips on staying focused in the body when stress strikes. ~Chapter 7 describes healthy boundary setting in personal encounters, phone conversations, and technology-based interactions. ~Chapter 8 provides a road map of the body, helping pave the way to identify and change unhealthy patterns. ~Chapter 9 portrays an understanding of personal space and of its impact on moods and interactions with others. ~Chapter 10 describes ways of uniting with intuition and using it throughout the workday.

Each chapter discusses an important principle and provides personal experiences, client anecdotes, and at least one easy exercise to practice. Every exercise builds on the previous one and can be completed in a matter of moments when time is short, or enjoyed more fully when time allows. They can be done during lulls in your daily activities such as waiting for your computer to boot up, in line at a store, or on hold during a phone call. Taking a few moments to try these techniques can improve communication and problem solving in your life with little effort and without disrupting normal routines. People in any career field or workplace setting can and will benefit from using these quick, simple techniques.

Some people willingly decide to look within for a different approach. Others seem to be forced by stressful circumstances to look within for answers. In either instance it is important to acknowledge that the decision to look within ultimately leads to a deeper connection with all the different parts of yourself. Because some of these parts reside in the subconscious, you may be unaware of their agendas—many of which may not align with your conscious goals. Those that do not can hinder your progress and keep you unfocused. When you tap into your inner awareness, your subconscious and conscious parts come together, and you immediately feel more connected. Choosing to acquaint yourself with your inner senses is nothing short of deciding to become *whole*. Soon you will find that using your inner and outer senses together expands your awareness, transforming not only you but other people around you.

An important point to remember when starting this process is that anything you try on an inner level is accomplished by allowing, rather than pushing or controlling. Allowing life to flow through you may at first feel unusual, but soon you will find yourself working far more effectively. Because life is uncertain and ever changing, trying to control anything in your life is an illusion anyway.

Slowing down, finding your own rhythm, and establishing a reasonable pace at the start of a busy workday is a different approach. With this approach, you can intuitively know when to move forward, when to pause and reflect, and most importantly, when to stop working and to allow your body to rest. The payoff is less stress, recognition of more opportunities, and the ability to realize your highest potential.

Chapter One

Focus

You're searching for your mind
Don't know where to start
Can't find the key
To fit the lock on your heart.
You think you know
But you are never quite sure...
— Ozzy Osborne

During a busy workday we are constantly bombarded by a variety of demands, decisions, and deadlines. The more we mentally focus on what we need to do, the more overwhelmed we can feel. Sometimes it may seem like we are trudging through the trenches, trying to accomplish our daily tasks without much enthusiasm or enjoyment.

In this day and age, we tend to be a highly mentally focused society. When stress or a crisis arises, it often seems safer to confront a problem mentally than to deal with our emotional reactions to it. However, in doing this, we cut ourselves off from the broader resources that are available to us through inner awareness.

Understanding the benefits of switching from a mental focus to a whole body awareness can fundamentally change your outlook, helping you accomplish what you need by using a more subtle yet more effective approach.

When you shift your focus from your mind to another part of your body, something powerful happens. Suddenly your mind releases control, and senses located throughout the body become immediately available to you. Because these senses work together to absorb and process the information around you, you then have more parts collaborating to solve problems instead of only your overworked mental center. In essence, you are changing from a mental focus to a whole-body awareness.

Imagine coming home with a brand new computer that has a variety of programs and options. If you do not take time to familiarize yourself with all the options and use only one or two of the programs available, you will end up utilizing only a small portion of its potential to make your work easier.

Similarly, keeping your focus in the mind limits your ability to experience and understand what is happening around you. However, as soon as you shift your focus from your overworked mental center, your awareness automatically expands. You are then able to use senses and insights you innately possess but have not been able to consciously employ for your benefit. Since your physical body's natural state is to work together as a whole, if you use your entire body as one processing center, you can deal with problems confronting you in a healthier and more rational manner. Becoming more aware of how tired your physical body is, you will also know when it is time to call it a day.

- Head-to-Heart -

Where should you move your focus? A powerful place to refocus for personal interactions is in the middle of your chest—your heart center. Daily interactions become more meaningful and successful if you focus on your heart center. When you speak from your heart, you are aligning with your personal truth. Placing a hand over your heart during a conversation is a great physical reminder to speak from your heart. No matter who you are dealing with—an angry customer, a demanding boss, or upwardly mobile coworkers who see you as an obstacle to their advancement—speaking from the heart resolves conflicts because you are coming from your personal truth. Although you cannot not change others, you can change yourself. Such refocusing eliminates unhealthy patterns of communication, provides a means to increased understanding, and gives everyone involved a neutral place to communicate.

Changing your focus from head to heart is an easy process. Sit back for a moment, place your hand at the center of your forehead, close your eyes, and imagine your mental focus beneath your hand. Picture it transforming into an orange ball of energy. If you can't picture it, then feel it or just know it is there. Now move the same hand to the middle of your chest and imagine the orange ball of energy there. Feel the energy around your chest. Speak from your heart and others will respond differently, because you are coming from your personal truth.

I had been divorced for two years when I found myself having major difficulties with a coworker. This person and I did not mesh from the start. We had very different orientations. He communicated from his mental center, relying on logic, while I came from emotions and feelings. After a few encounters, I found myself responding to him in the same way I had done in the past while communicating with my ex-husband. Since his words seemed to bring me to tears so easily, it was very uncomfortable to be around him.

To cope with the situation, I decided to focus in my heart center whenever I communicated with him, placing my hand at my heart as a physical reminder to come from there. After a few conversations, I noticed an amazing change in the way we were interacting. In shifting my focus to my heart center, I had provided both of us with a safe place to communicate with each other. From the start, I knew I had to change *my* old pattern of communicating, not *his*. Later, I realized that this man had unknowingly helped me heal some issues remaining from my divorce. After a while, we were able to establish trust with each other. To this day, although we are not close friends, I respect this person for who he is, and I think he would say the same about me.

Focusing on the heart center allows you to disengage from old patterns and conflicts. It also opens new and neutral avenues for communication, resolution of past issues, and problem solving.

A substance abuse counselor has this to say about changing his focus: "When I come from my heart center, I feel less fearful, am able to express myself more clearly, and am more assertive while communicating with clients and staff."

Speaking from your heart can also make presentations more effective. Standing in front of coworkers or a room full of strangers with diverse orientations can be a stressful experience for even the most experienced speaker. You can reach some of your audience with a mental focus, others with an emotional focus, and still others with a powerful approach. However, you can reach *everyone* with a presentation that comes from the heart center. When you speak from the heart, you are more focused and able to express yourself more fully because you are coming from your personal truth.

A keynote speaker who practiced changing his focus before an important presentation said: "Speaking from my heart during the presentation helped me focus and effectively communicate my ideas. I also surprised myself by not having to use my notes."

Throughout your body, you have inner and instincts just waiting to be activated. When you shift your focus from head to heart, these senses work together to absorb and process the information around you. You then have more of your parts working together to find solutions to problems, instead of relying only on the already overworked mental center. This refocusing frees up your psyche and allows your entire body to work in a more integrated manner.

An appraiser, speaking of both himself and his wife notes: "Our job, as you can imagine, is very detail-oriented and can be very stressful. When we start the day connecting with our hearts, our heads aren't pounding by the end of the day, and we find it easier to focus and pay attention to the big picture."

Following is the first of fourteen inner awareness exercises. Any time you are working with inner awareness, remind yourself to trust your first inkling, hunch, or insight. Most of us have at some time taken a multiple choice test that included a question we were unsure of. Suddenly, we had a hunch, a feeling, or a gut response that made us feel we knew the right answer. Our logical self then took charge, and we began analyzing every choice, causing us to dismiss our insight as inaccurate. When doing the exercises in this book, allow yourself to experience sensations *without* judging. Even though your logical part will make its presence known, pay attention to your first response.

If you watch animals, children, or older people in tune with nature, you will notice that they naturally rely on their intuition and insights. They know how to be spontaneous and use their vivid imaginations. Likewise, use your imagination and play with these exercises. They can be done during lulls in your daily activities—while stuck in traffic, or waiting in an airport for a delayed flight. In this way, you can improve communications and problem solving with little effort and without disrupting normal routines.

Head-to-Heart Exercise

Key phrase: "Head to heart"
Remember to allow this exercise to happen, rather than forcing it.
When you sit back, relax, and experience, everything will flow to you.

~Select a person with whom you have difficulty communicating.

~Talk to this person in your usual way, noting how your body feels during the conversation.

~Before your next interaction with this individual, move your focus from your head to your heart.

> Close your eyes and place your hand in the center of your forehead. Imagine your mental focus is located there. Picture your mental focus transforming into an orange ball of energy. If you can't picture it, then feel it or know it is there.

> Next, place your hand in the middle of your chest and imagine the orange ball of energy moving there. (Skip putting your hand here if this feels awkward.)

~Speak to the person from your heart center during the next interaction.

~Compare the two interactions. How did each one feel to you? Did the other person respond differently to the second interaction?

Quick version: Say to yourself, "Head to heart." Place your hand on your heart if you need a physical reminder to focus there.

In personal interactions, if you shift your focus from head to heart and speak from your heart, communication will be more effective and satisfying.

- Achieving Whole-Body Awareness -

Most of us think we have no spare time in our busy schedule. The thought of taking time to try something new, however potentially beneficial, may seem out of the question. If we take stock of the amount of time we are stuck in traffic, in a line at a store, or waiting for a client who is already a half hour late, we may realize we do have extra time in our busy day. Taking a few moments to be aware of our body during such times can be much more beneficial than becoming impatient and stressed while delayed.

To begin a quick check of your body, pick an area that feels tight, stressed, or in pain. Close your eyes and move your focus (in the form of an orange ball) to the stressed area. Allow the orange color to permeate this area for a few moments. The color orange is a calming healing energy that can absorb any tension or stress that is lodged in the body. Let the orange calm and relax the area as you take a few gentle breaths.

When a portion of the body is tense or in pain, most people tend to isolate it. A simple way to reintegrate the area is by moving your focus into it, allowing the orange energy to absorb whatever tension or pain is there. Shifting your focus to an area you have neglected, and allowing energy to flow through it, promotes the unified interaction of all parts of the body. Your body can then work together to feel whole again.

The following exercise demonstrates how you can take a moment during daily down-time and move your focus around your body, relaxing tense areas with calming orange energy.

Whole-Body Awareness Exercise

Remember to allow this exercise to happen, rather than forcing it.
As you sit back and relax, experience
the flow of energy in your body.

~Sit back and close your eyes.

~Place your hand in the center of your forehead and imagine your mental focus there. Picture your mental focus transforming into an orange ball of energy. If you can't picture it, then feel it or know it is there.

~Now, move your hand to the middle of your chest and imagine the orange ball of energy moving there.

~Become aware of how your chest is feeling. Is it feeling tight, calm, heavy, tingling, or painful? Allow the orange color to permeate this area. Take a few gentle breaths, allowing the area to relax with each breath. The color orange is a calming healing energy that can absorb tension or stress in the body.

~Now, allow your focus to move to the middle of your stomach. How does this area feel? Let the orange soak into this area while taking a few gentle breaths.

~Next, move your focus to your knee. How is your knee feeling? Move your focus to the other knee and compare the two.

Remember to allow your focus to move around your body during the day. Take note of how the different areas feel. Relax any tense areas with the orange color. Moving your focus to an area you have neglected allows energy to flow through it. Your body will then work as a whole again.

If your focus at any time shifts back to your head, focus again
on another area. With practice you can change from mental focus
to whole-body awareness.

Chapter Two

The Calm Center

As we let our own light shine, we unconsciously give
Other people permission to do the same.
As we are liberated from our own fear,
Our presence automatically liberates others.
—Marianne Williamson

Have you ever experienced a time in your life when everything you formerly relied on was in total chaos, and when you tried to remedy the situation it only became worse? When life becomes chaotic, most of us despair and try to quickly remedy the situation. However, when we react this way, we may miss the point of the whole experience. Now is the time to look within and view the situation from a different perspective, using our inner awareness. Often, adversity comes into our life to make way for new beginnings and change what is obsolete. Clinging to old patterns can prevent us from growing. If we resist such changes to keep the status quo, we may miss important opportunities life is offering.

For example, suppose you walk into work Monday morning only to be greeted by your boss demanding to know when the reports that aren't due until Friday will be ready. Later, at the water cooler, where you are looking for empathy from your coworkers, you find them grouchy and unsympathetic. To top off the morning, you check your messages and learn that you have just lost one of your most important accounts to a rival firm. The work environment that felt stable and rewarding last Friday now feels like a war zone.

Adversity challenges us to look within and become more creative and adaptable in discovering solutions to problems. In doing this we may also be forced to deal with parts of ourselves that we have not developed in the past. These challenges might seem like roadblocks in our path, and may not go away for a while.

When adversity strikes, you can go within and find the quiet, safe place that everyone possesses, your calm center. Taking time to connect with this center will separate you from chaos long enough to discover the clarity you need to resolve your dilemma. You might need to work on communication, become more of a team player, learn to set limits, or find a calm refuge and endure.

- Our Inner Core -

The calm center is located in the inner core, which runs from the top of your head to the base of your spine. The inner core is the clear intuitive part of the psyche that contains your goals, purpose, and highest potential. This knowing part of you understands who you are, why you came here, and what your purpose is.

The way to enter your inner core, or calm center, is through the heart. Do this by shifting your focus from head to heart. Placing your hand at your heart keeps your focus there and engages your calm center. You can then imagine a candle's flame entering your heart, lighting up your inner core. Start the process by saying out loud from your heart, "Trust." Expressing a word from your heart turns a mental thought into your personal truth.

This simple step is one of the most important discoveries I have come across. When you take a thought, light up your inner core, and express the thought from your heart, you are enlisting your clear intuitive part. Such a collaboration is powerful. When you ask for trust, your clear knowing part will respond, and you will feel the trust you need from deep within you. As the flame enters your heart and lights up your inner core, your core light surrounds you, melting away all the stress, fears, and doubts.

Connecting with your calm center and inner core is like experiencing the calm eye of a hurricane. The calm center allows you to separate from chaos. When the whirl of daily activities and accompanying stress makes you feel dizzy, you can engage your calm center and light up your inner core. Entering this place creates a healthy boundary between you and the chaos, and provides a means of renewal. Moreover, getting in touch with the inner core connects you with the intuitive part of you discussed in chapter 10.

You can compare the inner core, or calm center, to a lighthouse shining its bright beam to guide ships to safety on a turbulent sea. Your calm center is always there, illuminating the way to shore. Your inner core can connect you with your inner security in times of stress or crisis. For example, you may have had the wrenching experience of losing a job in a career field you've been in for a while and faced deciding whether to look for a position in the same profession or try something new. You may realize there is not much challenge in the "secure" occupation, but feel the idea of a new career unstable and risky. Connecting with your calm center will provide the trust and confidence you may need to start a new venture.

In addition, inner core light is also a very effective tool to increase self-esteem. Most people don't know how to love and accept themselves. In my own experience, there were days I felt great about myself and other days when I didn't want to leave the house.

Now when I feel this way, I connect with my calm center and light up my inner core. As the inner core becomes illuminated, it surrounds me, melting away all my stress, fears, and doubts. I take a deep breath, and as I breathe out, the inner core light spreads out and shines through my entire body, creating a 360 degree radius. I can sit for a few moments and experience this transformation. When I feel the light of my highest potential around me, I am ready to face a busy day at work.

The calm center not only transforms you but also affects others. When the light of your inner core radiates through you, other people you come in contact with are influenced by it even if they are not aware of it.

Imagine a disgruntled client or fellow worker feeling better after an encounter with you simply because you took time that day to shine your inner light around you. Instead of feeling drained by the encounter, your boundary made others feel uplifted as a result of being in your presence.

I first experienced this phenomenon when I was teaching an inner awareness class in which we took turns radiating and expanding energy so that each person in the room could feel it. After the exercise, everyone was amazed by how good they felt with their own energy surrounding them and how this energy positively affected others in the group. One man's energy was so peaceful we all joked that we must be in the presence of a holy man. To this day, I still remember how his core energy made us all feel. The more I work with inner awareness, the more I realize that lighting up my inner core and sitting in my calm center creates a trust in myself that becomes increasingly stronger. I would much rather be surrounded by my highest potential all day than by stress, doubt, or fear.

A computer network technician instructor who regularly uses the calm center exercise during classes says: "I deal with sixty students a day who are new to this profession. In their excitement to learn, they often repeat the same questions. When I feel myself becoming frustrated, I take a moment to connect with my calm center. I can then respond to their questions in a polite and appropriate way."

A natural therapist who does health assessments based on acupuncture points and muscle testing explains: "Before greeting clients, I light up my inner core. Doing this creates a trust within me, I find myself guided to their problem areas, and I can then help them attain their natural state of health and well-being."

Calm Center Exercise

Key phrase: "Head to heart...trust"
Remember to allow this exercise to happen, rather than forcing it.
When you sit back, relax, and experience, everything will flow to you.

~Sit back and close your eyes.

~Allow your focus to move from head to heart.

~Imagine a candle in front of you.

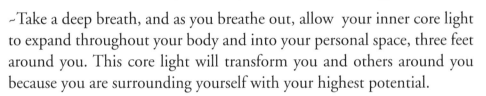

~Imagine the candle's flame entering your heart, lighting up your core. Start the process by placing your hand at your heart, and saying out loud from your heart, "Trust." Saying a word from your heart turns a mental thought into a personal truth.

~Take a deep breath, and as you breathe out, allow your inner core light to expand throughout your body and into your personal space, three feet around you. This core light will transform you and others around you because you are surrounding yourself with your highest potential.

Quick version: Say, "Head to heart." Place your hand at your heart and then from your heart say, "Trust." Take a breath and allow your inner core light to surround you.

When you feel off center during the day, you can renew the connection with your core by shifting your focus from head to heart and saying from your heart, "Trust." Your inner core light will expand around you.

- Be Like the Buddha -

At the start of a busy workday, it sometimes seems like we have just been let out of the starting gate, and we're off and running. From morning till evening, we are rushing here and there, making appointments and numerous phone calls, up to our elbows in paperwork and yellow stickies. We chase after what we think we need to accomplish, but the faster we run, the further away these accomplishments seem. We may realize by the end of such a day, that we have not taken any time to enjoy life. If the day that flew by turned out to be the last day of our life, would we be satisfied with how it was spent?

Fortunately there is a better, saner way to start a busy workday. This method employs the inner core, or calm center, discussed previously, as well as the philosophy of the Buddha. The simple act of sitting in your calm center, will change your pattern of chasing after what you need. When you take a few moments in the morning to sit in your calm center, you slow down enough to become part of life's flow and attract what you need in your workday.

A perfect example of understanding and utilizing life's flow is the philosophy of the Buddha. The Buddha resides in the center of life and allows the flow of life to provide all that is needed. Like the Buddha, when you change your focus from head to heart, light up your inner core, and sit in your calm center, life's flow can bring you the help you need throughout the day. Positive encounters such as running into the right person, having someone offer to help, or finding the perfect parking space will occur more frequently when you exist within and utilize life's flow.

The idea of sitting still and centering may create revolt in the conscious mind. Every miscellaneous thought that has been lurking in the background seems to spring forward and want your attention. The mind is so used to being in control that the very thought of being still can send the mind into overload.

You can avoid this problem by shifting your focus from your head to your heart. This refocusing allows you to disengage from mental chatter. Your mind can continue whatever mental antics it desires, but because your focus has been shifted to a different area, you will not be affected.

To attract what you need in your day, use the same steps from the previous chapters. Shift your focus from head to heart, automatically engaging your calm center. Then light up your inner core by placing your hand at your heart and saying, "Trust"—thus turning a mental thought into personal truth. Take a deep breath, and as you exhale, your inner core light will shine through your entire body, creating a 360 degree radius surrounding you. Next, take a few moments to sit like the Buddha and align yourself with life's flow. You can then attract what you need during the day to accomplish your tasks.

Here is an example of how this process can operate. When beginning to write this book, I realized how important it was to have a computer at home. I had a computer at work, but to make any progress I also needed to write at home. Although I did not think I had enough money to buy a computer, I decided not to let this stand in my way. First thing in the morning, I moved my focus from head to heart, lit up my inner core, sat in my calm center, and became like the Buddha. I continued sitting there for a few moments to attract what I needed and then went on my way and forgot about it. A few days later, I ran into a good friend who owed me a trade for some classes I had taught him. He said he had a surprise for me and came over that night with a laser printer. While he was there, he also mentioned he was going to a computer show that weekend and would look around for a computer for me. I had just received a bonus of $300 from work, so I gave him the money and wished him luck. That night I received a phone call letting me know I was now the proud owner of a brand new computer he had bought me with the money. I was now set up with a computer at home and had no excuse for not finishing this book.

A sales executive who uses the Buddha exercise to deal with daily stress reports: "At certain times during my day I have at least four people standing at my desk and another person on the phone. Everyone needs an answer, and they all need it *now.* I glance down and notice the little laughing Buddha sitting on my desk. I reach over and put my thumb on his belly, remembering to move my focus from head to heart and connect with the universal flow. Speaking from my heart addresses the chaos around me, and I answer all their questions. By the time I am done, the chaos has dissipated and I feel calm again."

Most people underestimate the power of just *being*. We live in such an aggressive and busy society that it seems foreign to take a few moments to connect with ourselves and life's flow. However, if we do take the time to light up our inner core and sit in our calm center, life's flow will be felt and utilized. Centering ourselves by becoming like the Buddha is a most powerful place to reside, one we should visit often.

Buddha Exercise

Key phrase: "Head to heart, be the Buddha, trust"
Remember to allow this exercise to happen, rather than forcing it.
When you sit in your calm center like the Buddha,
everything will flow to you.

~Sit back and close your eyes.

~Allow your focus to shift from head to heart.

~Imagine a candle in front of you.

~Imagine the candle's flame entering your heart, lighting up your core. Start the process by placing your hand at your heart, and saying out loud from your heart, "Trust." Saying a word from your heart turns a mental thought into a personal truth.

~Take a deep breath, and as you breathe out, the light of your inner core will expand throughout your body and into your personal space, three feet around you. This core light will transform you and others around you because you are surrounding yourself with your highest potential.

~Take a few moments to sit like the Buddha and align yourself with life's flow. In doing this, you will attract what you need to accomplish your tasks.

Quick version: Say, "Head to heart, be the Buddha," placing your hand at your heart, and then say from your heart, "Trust." Take a breath and allow your inner core light to surround you. Sit for a few moments to align with life's flow, and go on your way knowing you will attract what you need.

When you feel off center during the day, you can renew the connection with your core and life's flow by shifting your focus from head to heart, sitting like the Buddha, and saying, "Trust" from your heart.

Chapter Three

Intention

Live with intention
Walk to the edge
Continue to learn
Play with abandon
Choose with no regret
Laugh
Do what you love
Live as if
This is all there is.
—Marianne Radmacher-Hershey

When we first started the job or career we are in today, most of us were full of optimism. We chose our profession for a variety of reasons—to make money, achieve a goal—take the next step in the direction we wanted to go, or contribute to society. Our intentions in this field may have been as lofty as rising to the top of the corporate ladder, or as simple as earning a healthy salary so we could pay our bills.

Daily goals and intentions are an important component of your workday because they allow you to prioritize, stay inspired, and keep focused. Long-term goals help you see the bigger picture and keep you on track, with the knowledge that if you persevere, your effort will eventually pay off.

Since most of your waking time is usually spent at work, enjoying what you do for a living can make a big difference in your desire to get out of bed in the morning. Why? Because being in a career that inspires and fulfills you makes your life much richer.

Some of us have been lucky enough to find a profession that we truly enjoy, while others are still searching. Either way, we are in need of setting goals in our life. We all have a basic need to improve and better ourselves, whether it be materially, emotionally, mentally, or spiritually.

Writing down these goals, posting them in a conspicuous place, focusing on them, or repeatedly saying them are a few methods that often help us achieve goals. Yet sometimes goals take years to manifest or never materialize at all. There are several reasons for this. First, as a mentally focused society, most of us try to figure things out logically. When we send out our intentions or goals, we may be unconsciously holding on to them with our mental focus. Mentally focusing too much on our intentions or goals can keep us from reaching them quickly.

Second, most of us are surrounded by inhibiting or conflicting emotions. The achievement of our goals can be affected by whatever fears, doubts, or other negative emotions may be radiating in our personal space. Moreover, the negative energies and stress we pick up from people we interact with can also adversely affect our intentions. Energy in our personal space affects our ability to send a clear message about our goals or intentions to the universe.

A better approach to realizing your heart's desires is to place them in their rightful place—the heart center. The word *intention* begins with the syllable *in*, which means within. The heart center is where your personal truth resides. Lighting up your inner core connects you with your personal truth. Speaking your intention out loud from your heart changes your intention from a thought form to an expression of your personal truth, and also engages your clear intuitive part. This collaboration is powerful. When you ask for your intention or goal, your clear knowing part will respond, and you will feel the trust deep within you. If you sit quietly and allow your goal to permeate your entire being, it will become a part of you. You can then go about your day with the assurance that you will achieve your goal because the goal is now a part of you.

A good example of realizing an intention is how I acquired the house I now live in. For seven years I had been living in a small cabin overlooking a river, but I had to move since the owners were going to repair the cabin. I didn't know where I would end up; all I knew for sure was that I still wanted to live near the river. I wrote down what I wished for most in a new home—a two-story house by the river, with enough room for a garden. My teenage daughter wanted a house with two bathrooms, as she was tired of sharing one. Later that night, I moved my focus from head to heart, lit up my inner core, sat in my calm center, and like the Buddha, let the image of my ideal house become part of me. My daughter and I then took the description of our ideal house, folded it into a little boat, went outside, and placed it in the river. The very next day, I ran into a good friend of mine and asked if he knew of any houses to rent. He replied that the house next to his was for rent and told me to call him later. A day later I rented a two-story, two-bath home on the river, complete with a garden.

Setting a goal or intention at the start of a hectic workday makes total sense. Depending on the day, you may want help with balance, patience, organization, adaptability, or trust. You may also need to acquire something more concrete such as money, a job, housing, or a relationship. You can attract whatever you need by setting an intention or goal in your heart.

Pick a goal or intention that you wish to achieve in your life. Move your focus from head to heart, automatically engaging your calm center. Light up your inner core by placing your hand on your heart, and say from your heart, "Trust." Transform your intention or goal to an expression of your personal truth by either writing it down or saying it out loud from your heart. Allow the desire to permeate your entire body, and go on your way. Your intention or goal is now part of you, and you will attract what you need to succeed.

A saleswoman of many years states: "Being successful in this competitive field takes a lot of effort and time. In the past when I was tired or stressed, I would project too much energy towards my clients, which would tend to put them off. Now when I begin the day by setting my intentions in my heart, I attract what I need. My interactions with my clients have improved, and my sales have increased."

Whether we are aware of it or not, to a certain extent we create our own reality. Unfortunately, most of us do this unconsciously, with little thought about how conditions and situations might affect us and others. Because our thoughts are more powerful than we usually realize, we need to consider our options wisely and aim for the highest good when asking for something. To place an intention in the heart is to become a conscious creator, helping us attract what we need to reach our goals.

Intention Exercise

Key phrase: "Head to heart, be the Buddha, trust"
Remember to allow this exercise to happen, rather than forcing it. When you sit in your calm center like the Buddha, everything will flow to you.

~Sit back and close your eyes.

~Allow your focus to move from head to heart, which engages your calm center.

~Imagine the flame of a candle entering your heart, lighting up your inner core. Start the process by placing your hand at your heart and saying from your heart, "Trust." Saying a word from your heart turns a mental thought into a personal truth.

~Take a deep breath and allow your inner core light to expand throughout your body and into your personal space, three feet around you. Patience

~Sit like the Buddha and attract life's flow.

~Pick a goal or an intention and say it out loud from your heart center.

~Sit quietly for a few moments and allow the intention to permeate your entire being. Possible goals or intentions might be: patience, adaptability, organization, prosperity, balance, humor, integrity, perseverance, joy, a car, a job, wood for the winter, a date, or a vacation.

Quick version: Say, "Head to heart, be the Buddha," place your hand at your heart and say, "Trust." Next, say your intention or goal from your heart, or if you prefer, write it down.

When you have completed this exercise, know that wherever you go the universe will bring you your heart's desire, because it is safe within its rightful place—your heart center.

Chapter Four

Strength and Will

But the tides are always shifting,
The land is never still.
You cannot tame a river
And bend it to your will.
—Betsy Rose

We are taught from the time we are young to take action, control our thoughts, manage our time, and maintain self-control. These skills expected of us are not always easily acquired. We learn at a young age to enlist our will to deal with these demands.

By contrast, life teaches us different lessons—to let go, allow, take things in stride, and adapt, since circumstances are always changing and can be unpredictable. Life's flow can be summed up in the word, *strength*.

Strength can be compared to a flowing river that winds its way around obstacles, making them smooth with its constant motion. There are parts of the river that are very rough and dangerous, but there are also long stretches of calm water. Whether the water is rough or calm, the flow of the river, like the flow of life, is always there, spurring us on. If we start our workday connecting with the flow, the day's journey becomes as important as the destination.

Will, on the other hand, is like a train speeding down a track; its main purpose is its destination. If there is an obstacle in its way, the train might not be able to stop and could mow down whatever is on its tracks. Similarly, when our focus is on meeting our deadlines no matter what, we are attempting to control life and are not paying attention to its rhythms and cycles. Ironically, in trying to control life, we are limiting life. Pushing our way through our day's agenda as if we were on a mission can alienate people around us and cause us to miss significant opportunities.

Will is an important part of our psyche that is necessary for survival. When life feels scary and out of control, we often become inflexible to deal with our stress or fear. The more we react this way, the more we overuse our will to cope. Our situation becomes problematic when rather than using a combination of both strength and will, we overuse our will, ignoring the limits of our physical body. Living life exclusively through will can cause tension, stress, cancer, and related diseases.

Imagine your will as a mighty oak tree. Oak is very strong wood, but it is not at all flexible, and in heavy winds an oak tree can break. Strength, on the other hand, is like a supple reed, whose greatest asset is flexibility. If we use strength combined with will each day, it will be obvious when the load we're carrying is too much, since the reed will bend when the workload is overwhelming.

Beginning the day, lighting up your inner core and taking a few moments to sit in your calm center is an excellent way of connecting with life's flow and living through strength as well as will. Connecting with the flow at the start of a busy workday is a way of trusting that you will accomplish what is most important. Lighting up your inner core and sitting like the Buddha allows the flow to move through you all day. You will be able to change your direction if needed, instead of pushing to make sure everything on your day's agenda is completed. When you push, you create resistance and chaos around you, significantly slowing your productivity.

If you find yourself becoming stressed and inflexible about your day's agenda, you can stop and take a moment to reconnect with your inner core. This may seem difficult to do on a busy day, but connecting with life's flow can positively affect the entire day's outcome. As a result, you might, for example, bump into a person you have been trying to reach, or come up with the solution to a problem you've been trying to solve. Such things can happen when you are centered enough to recognize opportunities that the flow is presenting. You can see circumstances change on an outer level by connecting with the flow on an inner level.

A significant aspect of strength is trusting adversity. At times life is difficult, unmanageable, and seems like more than one person can handle. However, if you shift your focus from head to heart when chaos strikes, and not make hasty judgments, you will find that life's flow is always working in the midst of the chaos. Experiencing chaos is like paddling into white-water rapids. Staying calm, paying attention, listening, and hanging on might be all you can do. Whether or not you stay in the boat, you must trust that you can handle the experience and count on calm water ahead.

Don't get me wrong, your will does not need to go away. While your will is necessary to meet life's challenges, connecting with the flow and lighting up your inner core can create a better balance between strength and will.

If your day seems like it is spinning out of control, sit back for a moment and close your eyes. Shift your focus from head to heart, engaging your calm center. Place your hand at your heart and light up your inner core by saying from your heart, "Trust." Sit like the Buddha to attract life's flow. Allow your hands to rest on your desktop or lap, with your palms facing the ceiling. Imagine the palms of your hands opening up wide. Picture a river entering your palms and running throughout your body and out your feet. Start the process by saying out loud from your heart, "Flow." Take a deep breath and imagine a river flowing into your hands and through your entire body. Continue for a few moments breathing deeply and picturing the river. Life's flow will balance your will with strength.

Soon after I became divorced, I made the decision to learn to live through strength, and trust life to provide what I needed. This meant I would make a conscious effort to live in the flow. It seemed like a good choice at the time, since I didn't have much to lose materially with only part-time jobs and not much money. That summer, I rented a small cabin on a river, and became a river guide. In retrospect, I can see life gave me a front-row seat to study a perfect symbol of strength—the river.

Since then, the river has seemed to mirror my life. During my first summer as a river guide, I learned to look ahead to see where I wanted to position my boat. In my life as well, I had to look ahead to see what direction I wanted to take. I knew I wanted to work with children, and that fall I found a job teaching in a home study program.

Each year since then, I have learned new lessons from the river. One year was a low-water season with rocks in the river I had never noticed before. Similarly, in my personal life and at work it seemed all I dealt with were obstacles. Another year I was attempting to hold down three jobs to make ends meet, on the verge of falling apart physically, mentally, and emotionally. At that point of desperation, I made an important if not obvious realization: if I continued trying to cope using only my will, I wouldn't last much longer. I decided I would somehow reduce my workload and slow down so I could keep my sanity. The next thing I knew, I was laid off from one of my jobs. It seemed the decision of how to go about slowing down my life was out of my hands. This was certainly not the way I would have changed things, but the experience helped me learn to trust adversity. As it turned out, I survived financially, was able to be a sane mother, and learned to appreciate the concept of allowing life to work through me. Having one less job allowed me to slow down enough to attract what I needed, instead of pushing myself beyond my limits to finish everything.

Unfortunately, last year's flood washed away a lot of debris in the river, including my little cabin. Luckily, I had moved the previous year, and by then was living in a home 150 feet from the river's edge. That year, I was very glad to be part of life's flow instead of in the way of the river's flow.

A former insurance risk manager's anecdote: "My wife had just started an inner awareness course. After a few weeks, I began to notice a transformation in her. I decided to share in these changes, so I started the course a few months later. In the first couple of classes, we learned about the different aspects of strength and will, the quality of the journey being as important as the destination. I was working as a risk manager at the time, and every Monday morning I would start work with a severe headache. The class helped me realize that I was using my will to cope with my stressful job. After I acknowledged and worked with my will part, the headaches disappeared. Soon after, I made the decision to change my career and become more proactive instead of reactive in my life. I changed jobs and now work in education."

Always life challenges us to remember to experience what we did naturally when we were younger. By slowing down and finding our own pace we begin to work within life's balance. In allowing strength to become an important part of our day, we commit to connect with and utilize the flow, trusting we will accomplish what is most important while still enjoying our day.

Strength and Will Exercise

Key phrase: "Head to heart, be the Buddha, trust-flow."
Remember to allow this exercise to happen, rather than forcing it. When you
sit in your calm center like the Buddha, everything will flow to you.

~Sit back and close your eyes.

~Allow your focus to move from head to heart engaging your calm center.

~Sit in your calm center like the Buddha, attracting life's flow.

~Picture the flame of a candle entering your heart. Imagine the flame expanding throughout your inner core. Say out loud from your heart, "Trust."

~Allow your hands to rest on your desktop or lap, with your palms facing the ceiling. Imagine the palms of your hands opening up wide.

~Picture a river entering your palms and running throughout your body and out your feet.

~Sit in your calm center and say out loud from your heart, "Flow."

~Relax and receive life's flow. Take a few deep breaths, all the while imagining a river flowing through your entire body. Life's flow will balance your will with strength. If you have more time, allow the flow to run through you until your entire body feels fluid.

Quick version: From your heart say, "Head to heart, be the Buddha, trust." Place your hands on your desk or lap, palms facing the ceiling, and from your heart say, "Flow."

Try this exercise when you are feeling rigid
or when you need to feel life's flow.

Chapter Five

Energy

There is a muscular energy in sunlight
corresponding to the spiritual energy of wind.
—Annie Dillard

To keep up with today's fast pace, most of us push our physical body beyond its limits, depleting its energy supply. When we run out of energy, we may turn to artificial stimuli for help, using caffeine, nicotine, drugs, alcohol, or adrenaline—anything except what is free and always available, earth energy and potential energy. Earth and potential energy are inexhaustible sources of free fuel that our physical body can draw from all day long. Running on this mix of energies is not new; utilizing these energies is what our body was originally designed to do. As children, we naturally tapped into these energies; we felt connected to the earth, trusted the universe, and were part of life's flow.

Running on our physical body's limited energy can be compared to homes powered by nonrenewable resources, such as coal, nuclear energy, or oil. These homes have a reliable power source, but there is a downside to using such power sources. Homes powered by these means use the earth's limited energy resources, and come with a monthly bill. When we push our body beyond its limits and deplete our body's limited energy resources, we may not pay a monthly bill, but down the road we may end up paying lots of medical bills.

Using earth and potential energy as our energy source is similar to homes relying on wind or solar power—free and inexhaustible energy resources from nature. With these resources, there is no depletion of the earth's natural resources and the power source is free.

Since depleting our body's limited resources can ultimately lead to stress and disease, it makes sense to use the free and renewable energy resources of earth and potential energy. This blend of energies calms and energizes the body, reconnecting us with the earth and allowing us to experience life's flow.

- Earth Energy -

Earth energy is a warm, calm, dense energy that originates in the core of the earth. It enters the physical body through the feet and flows throughout us. This energy is the conduit that provides the connection and support our physical body needs on a daily basis. Working indoors separates us from our natural connection with earth energy. However, even if we are lucky enough to have an outdoor job, we may be so rushed during the day that we are unable to connect with the earth and receive the energy our body needs. Sitting quietly and allowing earth energy to flow into our feet and throughout our body neutralizes anxiety and tension. We are then able to listen to our body's needs, regain our balance, and feel life's flow.

- Potential Energy -

Potential energy is a light, airy energy that comes from the universe. It enters the body through the crown of the head, flowing throughout us and transforming blocked energy into moving energy again. This transformation allows our body to feel lighter and more fluid. Moreover, potential energy enflames our imagination and creative processes, providing the inspiration we need to manifest our vision and goals.

- Mixing Energies -

Earth energy feeds and supports the physical body, providing the fuel our body needs on a daily basis. Potential energy is the spark that ignites and inspires creativity. Allowing these two energies to merge and flow throughout our body will create the flame needed to light our inner core. Our clear intuitive part is now active and can create a balance between the body and mind.

- Energy Imbalances -

An imbalance of either earth energy or potential energy can affect us in a variety of ways. Such an imbalance may determine how our body copes with stress, if we are able to meet our needs, and ultimately, what our lessons in life will be.

- Earth Energy Imbalance -

If you have a strong connection with potential energy but lack earth energy, you will deal with stress by partially leaving your body. Since your body is not anchored strongly to the earth and you have a strong connection with potential energy and the universe, your physical body won't feel stable enough for your psyche. When you experience that spacy, out-of-control feeling at the end of the workday, know that your focus has left due to stress.

A lack of earth energy and a weak connection with the earth can adversely affect your ability to meet your basic needs, because your body does not feel support from the physical world. A job, money to pay bills, and a roof over your head are necessities that do not come naturally for people with a lack of earth energy.

Personally, I have always felt a strong connection with potential energy and had a weak connection with the earth. In stressful situations, because my body did not feel the support of the earth I would tense up and barely breathe. As I tensed up, my personal boundaries would retract, allowing whatever was bothering me to come closer. Because my body was so uncomfortable, I would soon feel detached from it—a condition that interfered with my concentration, organizational skills, and personal relationships. My body then became even more stressed with anxiety.

Because of my strong connection with potential energy, I have always had a basic trust in the future and a strong connection with the universe. As a result, I was able to learn to meditate very easily, have a lot of imagination, and am in touch with my intuition.

To achieve better balance between earth energy and potential energy, these days I spend time connecting with the earth. I allow earth energy to relax me so I can stay in my body in stressful situations. Starting my day powered by both earth and potential energy, I find I have sufficient stamina to see me through. I am supported by the earth and feel more stable in all areas of my life. Moreover, I have been able to discover practical ways to implement my ideas in my career. Writing this book is part of my manifestation.

- Potential Energy Imbalance -

People who have a strong connection with earth energy but lack potential energy, tend to have a secure base and are able to stay in their bodies in stressful situations. However, without a lot of potential energy flowing through them, their bodies might become heavy and dense, causing them to lose sensitivity to their instinctual responses and needs.

People with this kind of imbalance would benefit from more potential energy flowing through them. This would make their bodies feel lighter and more fluid, and would increase their awareness of their work environment and of interactions with others. Potential energy helps manifest the vision, goals, and inspiration needed to unite everyone with their higher purpose.

These are just two examples of earth energy and potential energy imbalances. Because everyone is unique, people at various times may have either of these imbalances or a combination of both. What is most important to remember is when you allow in equal amounts of both types of energy, you will find a balance between your psyche and physical body, feel more safe and secure no matter what situations life brings, and be able to connect with your highest goals throughout your life.

To better connect with these two free neutral energies, in the morning before getting out of bed, take a moment to move your focus from head to heart. Sit like the Buddha to attract life's flow. Place your hand on your heart and say out loud from your heart, "Trust-flow," to start the flow of energies. The two energies will mix together and light up your inner core. Next, take a deep breath, and as you exhale, expand your inner light around you. This process only takes a few moments. You can then start your day powered by a free neutral energy source.

Any time you feel knocked off center during the day, renew your connection with the energies by placing your hand at your heart, and saying out loud or silently, "Head to heart, be the Buddha, trust-flow." Take a deep breath, and as you exhale, your inner core light will expand around you.

In the words of a woman who has been dealing with chronic fatigue syndrome and hepatitis: "Connecting with earth energy and potential energy on a regular basis has helped me stabilize my body, improve my physical stamina, and start working. Added bonuses have been less mental fatigue, the ability to utilize my intuition during my workday, and the awareness to know when I am expending too much energy towards others."

From an artist, art teacher, and interior designer: "With the variety of jobs I do, I find myself wearing many hats. I teach a multitude of art classes, working with a diverse population that includes independent-study and high-risk students. My busy schedule was compounded two years ago, when I was diagnosed with an extremely rare form of cancer. As I was hit with this diagnosis, I felt detached from my body and my center, wondering whether I would be around in the immediate future. By connecting with earth and potential energy and relying on Mother Earth, I found the strength to survive the ensuing treatments. These energies calmed my body enough that I was able to reclaim my center and align with my inner self. It has been two years since this roller coaster began. I am now back at work part-time with a more manageable schedule, and am now cancer free."

You make the choice. Continuing to deplete your body's limited resources can ultimately lead to stress and disease, whereas running on a blend of earth and potential energy will calm and energize your physical body, and allow you to live in life's flow. And don't forget the best part—there is no monthly bill!

Daily Energy Exercise

Key phrase: "Head to heart, be the Buddha, trust-flow"
Start the day with this simple exercise. Remember to allow this exercise to happen, rather than forcing it. When you sit in your calm center like the Buddha, everything will flow to you.

~Sit back for a moment and close your eyes.

~Allow your focus to move from head to heart.

~Sit in your calm center like the Buddha, attracting life's flow.

~Picture the flame of a candle entering your heart. Imagine the flame expanding throughout your inner core. With your focus at your heart, say, "Trust."

~Next, connect with earth energy and potential energy by saying out loud from your heart, "Flow." Expressing this word from your heart will start the process. Earth energy will flow into you through your feet, while potential energy will flow through your crown. These two energies will mix together and light up your inner core, providing the energy needed for the day.

~Breathing deeply, allow your inner core light to expand around you.

Quick version: While lying in your bed in the morning, move your focus from head to heart, be like the Buddha, ask for the support from the earth and the universe, starting the flow of energies by saying, "Trust-flow."

During the day, if life knocks you off balance, renew your energy connection by saying, "Head to heart, be the Buddha, trust-flow."

Chapter Six

Grounding

The best remedy for those who are afraid, lonely or unhappy
is to go outside somewhere where they can be quiet,
alone with the heavens, nature and God.
Because only then does one feel that all is
as it should be, amidst the simple beauty of nature.
I firmly believe that nature brings solace in all troubles.
—Anne Frank

Our body is an incredible machine. We wake it up in the wee hours of the morning, fill it full of coffee, shove it out the door, and we're off to work. During our busy workday, we drag our body around behind us, stressing it with what seem like a million phone calls, meetings, and deadlines. Halfway through the day, when our body is exhausted, we ply it with caffeine, aspirin, and fast food, and then wonder why it can't keep up. When we think about it, our body does an amazing job coping with today's fast pace, although we sometimes push it too far.

In the past, survival was what life was all about. People spent most days hunting and foraging for food, which kept them in top physical condition. They listened to their body's instinctual responses, because often life depended on it. Since the majority of time was spent outdoors, they were naturally grounded and connected with the earth, and worked within life's balance.

By contrast, in modern times we spend most of our working days inside, surrounded with lots of noise, stress, and hectic schedules. As life's pace quickens, we lose the ability to stay in tune with our body's natural responses and our intuition. As we become increasingly less in tune with our body, it starts to resist stress and creates barriers to cope. These barriers can include weight gain, smoking, alcohol or drugs. Unfortunately, such barriers do not just affect those around us, they also affect our own relationship with our body. We may start to relate to our physical body as separate from us and cease listening to it when it is tired, rundown, or stressed.

Since your physical body's job is to protect you, your body is slower to embrace change than your psyche is. When your body encounters too much stress, it tends to react to any change, positive or negative, as a danger and resist it. You may be excited about a promotion, job change, or a move to a different location. Your body, on the other hand, might resist the change if it is under too much stress, and as a result gain weight, get sick, or have a nervous breakdown as a form of protection.

Grounding is renewing your connection with the physical body and the earth. If you start the day grounding your body with the earth, you will feel centered and able to respond to change and stress in a more efficient and healthier way. You will then remain more focused in your body instead of feeling disconnected. Moreover, grounding your body on a daily basis heightens your awareness of your body's needs. Consequently, you become attuned to your body's signals and are more alert at work.

First thing in the morning, before getting out of bed, take a moment to move your focus from head to heart, engaging your calm center. Next, sit like the Buddha to connect with life's flow. Since earth and potential energy can light up your inner core, the word trust *now takes on a new meaning. Saying the word* trust *from your heart engages the support of the earth in the form of a huge hand. Once you feel the support of the hand, and have established a trust with the earth, say from your heart, "Flow." The word* flow *starts earth and potential energy moving through your body, automatically lighting up your inner core. Saying a word from your heart turns a mental thought into your personal truth. Take a few breaths and*

allow your inner core light to expand around you. Then start your day pow-
ered by a free neutral energy source.

During the day, if stress has knocked you off center, take a moment to do
the quick version of this exercise by saying, "Head to heart, be the Buddha,
trust," and when you feel the support of the hand, say, "Flow." Then go about
your day with your body grounded and supported by the earth, and powered
by earth and potential energy. All this is done by allowing, not forcing. Then
your body and you are a powerful team that can work together to adapt to the
constant changes life brings.

- Grounding and Exercise -

Although exercise is a great way to release stress and stay clear mentally and emotionally, it is important to balance workouts with enough
time sitting on the ground. Like anything else, exercise can be overdone
and overused. Sometimes you force yourself to exercise when your body
really needs a break. When you take time to connect with earth, your
body can work together with your mind, and you will realize when to give
it a rest.

Sitting outside on the ground whenever possible is the best way to
renew your body and restore your sense of peace. If there is a park near
work, or even a small section of grass, or a tree in the parking lot where
you can sit, you can regain your sense of composure and help your body
cope. When you take time to sit on the ground, your body and psyche
will feel renewed.

One day I was sitting by the river and decided to lay down on the
bank and connect with the earth. No one was around other then a few
Canadian geese, so I felt comfortable lying by the water. I moved my
focus from head to heart, lit up my inner core, and became like the Buddha. I said, "Trust-flow," and felt myself connecting with the earth and
starting to relax. After about five minutes, I felt refreshed and decided to
walk back to my cabin. As I started to get up, I was startled to find that
the Canadian geese had moved very close and were nesting around me in
a half circle three feet away. While I had been lying down, I was so con-

nected with the earth, they may not have realized how close in proximity to me they were. I was so relaxed, I didn't hear them approaching. This experience doesn't say much for my survival skills, but it does show that when you connect with the earth, the resulting energy flow is felt by others, human or not.

When you take the time in the morning to ground and connect to earth and potential energy, people, like the geese, will be drawn to you, and you will attract what you need. Such grounding is especially helpful when dealing with irate customers, making a presentation, or closing an important deal.

- Grounding and Trauma -

Grounding is also essential when you are about to undergo any medical procedure. Since your body's job is to protect you, it may regard an operation or other medical procedure as a danger to you and offer resistance. Instead, you want your body to cooperate and help you heal. When you take the time to prepare it for a change by grounding it with the earth, your body can then deal with the change and go with the flow instead of resisting.

Similarly, a traumatic experience can knock you off balance and leave you feeling disconnected from your body. Grounding will calm your physical body so your psyche can return and feel secure again.

A few years ago, I was working on the river during a high-water season. A third of the way down the river, my crew and I noticed a woman clinging to a tree midstream. Another guide and I made it to shore and climbed upriver directly across from her. We were able to toss her a throw bag and pull her to shore. Since she was traumatized, I took her hand and asked if I could do a calming exercise with her, and grounded both of us with the earth. As a result, she calmed down and felt better and as an added bonus I calmed down as well.

If someone you know is upset or not feeling well, you can do a calming exercise with them. Take their hands in yours and move your focus from head to heart. Sit like the Buddha and from your heart say, "Trust." When you feel the support of the earth, say, "Flow." This starts earth energy and potential energy flowing through your body, which automatically lights up your inner core. The energy flows through you and into the person you are grounding, rejuvenating both of you simultaneously. The more you do nothing but focus on your heart, the more the earth can connect with and calm you both.

Similarly, if someone you know is going through a trauma and lives far away, you can picture the person in front of you, and send them the trust and energy they need to help them through their dilemma.

- Grounding and Animals -

Animals also need grounding at times, and are a lot easier to ground than humans. Once, some good friends of mine had just come home from a vacation to find their dog, Rocky, out of sorts. Rocky was howling a lot and did not want to go outside, in contrast to his usual behavior. He was still acting the same way the next morning, so they took him to a vet. Since the vet could find nothing physically wrong with him, they decided something must have scared him while they were on vacation, so together they grounded him with earth and potential energy. As a result, Rocky calmed down and was soon acting himself again.

The following exercise can be done quickly and will provide the support necessary during the workday. You can renew your connection with the earth whenever your busy schedule throws you off balance.

Grounding Exercise

Key phrase: "Head to heart, be the Buddha, trust-flow
Remember to allow this exercise to happen, rather than forcing it.
When you sit in your calm center like the Buddha,
everything will flow to you.

~Sit back and close your eyes.

~Allow your focus to move from head to heart, engaging your calm center.

~Sit in your calm center like the Buddha, attracting life's flow.

~Imagine the earth sending you support in the form of a huge hand. Allow this hand to ground your body by saying from your heart, "Trust." Feel total support from the earth.

~Next, connect with both earth energy and potential energy by saying out loud from your heart, "Flow." Expressing this word from your heart will start the process. Earth energy will flow into you through your feet, while potential energy will flow into you through your crown. These two energies will mix together and light up your inner core, providing the energy needed for the day.

~Breathing deeply, allow your inner core light to expand around you.

Quick version: Move your focus from head to heart, be like the Buddha, ask for the hand of support from the earth, and start the flow of energies by saying from your heart, "Trust-flow."

During the day, if you feel knocked off center or spacy, take a moment to reconnect with the earth by grounding your body.

- Grounding Living Spaces -

After working with energy for the past twelve years, I understand the importance of grounding and clearing any area that is constantly filled with our ever-changing emotions and energy. Everything and everyone is made up of energy. Homes, offices, cars, and the living space we inhabit collect energy from our interactions. Depending on the interactions, this energy can feel light and uplifting or heavy and debilitating.

A client once told me that she hated to walk into her office in the morning. The minute she entered the room she felt drained and tired. Her job involved overseeing a large firm with lots of stressful interactions among a variety of people, and apparently the emotionally charged energy seemed to hang in the air. However, when she started to ground and clear the energy in her office on a daily basis, right away she noticed the difference and felt better at work.

An interviewee recalls: "A few years ago I had an interview for a part-time job. After a few minutes of waiting, I got up and left. It wasn't fear of an interview that made me leave, even though I did feel nervous about it. The receptionist was friendly enough, and the decor of the office was pleasant. Instead, what made me uncomfortable was the atmosphere of the place itself. Sitting there, I felt suffocated by the energy of the office. I couldn't imagine working in a place with that kind of smothering feeling surrounding me. I now know earth energy and potential energy can change the atmosphere of any living space."

Imagine the difference that grounding can make in the workspace you inhabit. If there has been lots of stress and turmoil floating around your office, taking time to ground and clear the energy in the office would be doing everyone a favor—clients and workers alike.

When my daughter was little, she was afraid of the dark. She made up a little rhyme before she went to bed to help her feel safe during the night.

Over the years, I used her rhyme in my seminars with good results. It goes like this: "Mother Earth, ground me. White light surround me." Such an expression of grounding can make us all feel more secure and connected to the earth and the universe.

You can use the methods presented in the previous chapters to ground your office and home. Saying your key phrases, "Head to heart, be the Buddha, trust-flow" from your heart, and expanding your inner core light throughout the room or building, will transform the atmosphere of any physical space. If you prefer, you can adapt my daughter's rhyme: "Mother Earth, ground this car/room/office. White light surround this car/room/office."

Further, if during an important meeting, matters don't seem to be progressing, or there is tension in the air, you can say to yourself, "Trust-flow" or "Mother Earth..." This will alleviate the tension between individuals and facilitate progress in business negotiations.

A primary teacher has this to say about grounding her classroom in the morning: "The difference in my classroom's atmosphere is very apparent on the days I take a moment to ground my room. When I clear the energy left from the previous day's events, the students and I are more focused, the day's events goes more smoothly, and I feel good knowing I have provided a calm and safe environment to learn and share in."

"An environmental designer and feng shui practitioner notes: The grounding exercise has become an essential part of my business. I make sure I ground myself in the morning to give me focus and clarity during my workday. I then ground and clear the office space and other buildings I work in, sharing this valuable tool with my clients."

Grounding

Any room or office can be grounded to clear the atmosphere and facilitate the flow of energy. Walking into the office in the morning can be a more pleasant and productive experience when you ground your living space on a regular basis.

Grounding Living Space Exercise

Key phrase: "Head to heart, be the Buddha, trust-flow," or "Mother Earth, ground this car/room/office. White light surround this car/room/office." Remember to allow this exercise to happen, rather than forcing it. When you sit in your calm center like the Buddha, everything will flow to you.

~Sit back and close your eyes.

~Allow your focus to move from head to heart.

~Sit in your calm center like the Buddha, attracting life's flow.

~Imagine the earth sending up support in the form of a huge hand to the room you are sitting in. Allow this hand to ground the room/office/car by saying from your heart, "Trust."

~Next, allow the room to connect with both earth energy and potential energy by saying out loud from your heart, "Flow." Earth and potential energy will neutralize the energy of the room/office/car.

Note: If the room's energy is extremely dense, lighting a candle or burning some incense can help transform the atmosphere. Lavender or sage is always appropriate for clearing living spaces.

You can also change the atmosphere of a room during an important meeting. Move your focus from head to heart, place your hand at your heart center if needed, and say to yourself "Trust-flow." In response, the earth and energies will do their part to help stabilize interactions.

Chapter Seven

Boundaries

Don't ever take a fence down
until you know why it was put there.
—Robert Frost

In today's densely populated world, the term *boundaries* seems to be used more and more in our vocabulary. During a busy workday, we are exchanging energy with those around us, taking on each other's problems, stress, and anxiety. Without a healthy boundary, this exchange of energy can deplete the physical body and leave us feeling drained at the end of the day.

Boundaries are essential in every area of our lives—at work, at play, and at home. As small children, we learned the boundaries of parents and siblings, and later experienced boundaries with friends, classmates, and teachers. For me, however, there never seemed to be a tangible way to set boundaries until I began working with people's energy in my seminars. When I started teaching inner awareness classes, I noticed that I became more sensitive to energy, was able to feel different boundaries, and could tell where one person's energy stopped and another person's began. Because of this increased awareness, I discovered a discernible way to help others feel and establish healthy boundaries on an energy level.

As an example, one woman who attended my seminar had a prickly outer layer about an inch thick surrounding her personal space. However, underneath it was a warm, loving layer that more accurately reflected her identity. The problem was that most people reacted to her prickly outer layer, although if they stayed around her long enough, they found she was a warm, caring individual. During class, she expanded her inner core light and transformed her personal space using the "Trust-flow" method. Expanding her inner core light transformed the prickly outer layer into a neutral boundary, helping her radiate who she was rather than her defenses.

- Types of Boundaries -

Over the years, I have found that people have very different energy fields forming their boundaries. These energy fields run the gamut from feeling comfortable, to feeling prickly, weak, aggressive, or solid as a brick wall.

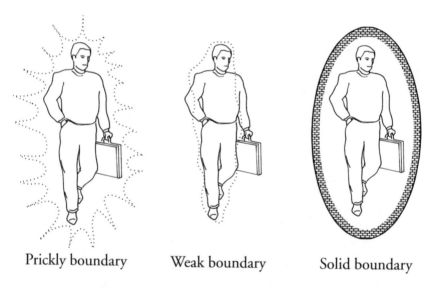

Prickly boundary   Weak boundary   Solid boundary

Weak or strong boundaries can correspond to various personality types or situations. Furthermore, people naturally expand their boundary when they are feeling good, retract it when feeling bad, or use it as a defense mechanism if feeling hurt or vulnerable. The point to remember is that your emotions are always reflected around you in your personal energy field.

People with a strong energy field surrounding them not only fill up their personal space but sometimes take up the space of those around them. For this reason they might need to learn how to pull in their boundaries at times. For example, while trying to get their point across in a conversation, they might unknowingly project their energy into another person's space, causing that person discomfort or unconsciously pressuring them. Giving others the space to express themselves can make a significant difference in such human interactions as connecting with a client, making a lasting sale, or creating a trust with a subordinate or a boss. Personal relationships improve greatly when you allow those around you to express themselves without taking up their personal space.

Conversely, people with a weak energy field tend to retract their energy field close to their bodies, especially in stressful situations. Such a reaction can adversely affect behavior. For example, people who react this way—often those with diminished self-confidence—have a hard time saying no to people with stronger personalities. However, as they learn to expand their energy around them, they feel more powerful and able to express themselves in a more assertive and healthy way.

Woman with weak boundary   Woman with strong boundary

- Boundaries and Our Emotions -

Did you ever wake up feeling angry, then push the anger aside in hopes of having a pleasant day in spite of how you felt? You no doubt noticed that people you encountered later in the day seemed angry. When an emotion is repressed or set aside, the feeling will permeate your personal space, affecting others in your world.

Boundaries continuously project our thoughts and feelings no matter how adept we are at masking them. When we are feeling upbeat and centered, the projected emotions can positively affect our interactions, while if we are impatient, pushy, or sad, these emotions can negatively affect others. People we come in contact might feel either uplifted or exhausted accordingly.

What can you do if you wake up and don't feel on top of the world? On days when you have no time to deal with feelings of anger, sadness, or vulnerability, rather than push these emotions aside and have others run into them, you can learn to neutralize them.

Take a moment to move your focus from head to heart, be like the Buddha, place your hand at your heart, and say, "Trust-flow." Then take a deep breath, and exhale while relaxing your inner core light around your body. This light will neutralize any emotions you have lingering in your personal space.

While surrounding you and your emotions, your inner light will create a healthy boundary that will act as a buffer zone between you and your coworkers. Over the course of the day, your inner core light will you own and neutralize any emotions in your personal space, transforming them into flowing energy again.

- Talk to the Hand -

Most people are not aware of all the energy impacting them as they go about their daily tasks. However, energy interactions in the workplace can affect everyone's energy level, leaving all coworkers exhausted by day's end. The constant energy exchange that goes on in a busy office takes a huge toll on your physical body leaving you with little energy left over for personal relationships.

Fortunately, there is a simple way to diffuse the steady stream of energy encountered during the day. Instead of letting it wear down your body, you can redirect the energy to your hand. This boundary can be used all the time or for special occasions when you know sparks are going to fly. Using your hand to deflect incoming energy establishes a healthy boundary around your body. In this way rather than taking on other people's stress and problems, you redirect the advancing energy, allowing them to "talk to the hand."

This technique calls for subtlety and discretion since having your hand in other people's faces is not a great way to make friends and influence people. Hence, here is a subtle way to redirect energy away from your body: Rest your hands on your desk, in your lap, or at your side. As you start a conversation, mentally direct the energy to your hand. Allow the energy to flow in and out of your hand in one smooth circular motion.

Holding a pen in your hand while talking to someone is also a great reminder to direct their energy toward your hand. With this in mind, I had a special boundary tool made as a reminder to set my boundaries throughout my day. It is: a snazzy little pen that says on it, "Talk to the hand."

When using this method of transferring energy, conversations might seem less engaging at first, but with only a little practice you will be as comfortable as when using your whole body as an energy receptor. When people blend too much on an energy level, they can take on each other's anger, frustration and hurt, which does not improve anyone's attitude. The benefits will become apparent when you have more energy for personal pursuits at the end of the day.

As I start a conversation, I hold a pen in my hand, or rest my hands on my desk or lap, as a reminder to direct the incoming energy toward my hand. I imagine the energy flowing into my hand and out in a constant circular motion. Redirecting the incoming energy of people around me helps me maintain a healthy boundary, and gives my body a much needed break.

A dental hygenist skilled in the use of boundary tools says: "Boundaries are crucial when your fingers are in other people's mouths all day long. People are very anxious when visiting the dentist office. Keeping their anxiety and energy at my hands allows me to be fresh for each new patient, and stops me from carrying fear and anxiety home to my family."

If you have been through trauma, and your heart center is in crisis, it is possible to set a healthy boundary without focusing on your heart. You can set a quick boundary by moving your focus from your head to your hand, then walk through the rest of your day.

A woman dealing with crisis had this to say: "I had just gone through a devastating breakup. Work was crazy, and of course my boss wanted everything done yesterday. I was at my breaking point, and all I wanted to do was to go somewhere quiet and cry. As I turned around, I remembered my tools. I didn't want to focus on my heart, because it was too full. Instead, I moved my focus to my hand and set my boundaries from there. I was able to keep everyone's energy out of my space and make it through the rest of the day."

- Boundaries and the Phone -

In almost any profession, the constant ringing of the phone can be a major annoyance. Moreover, cellular phones have expanded communication, making it possible to be available twenty-four hours a day. Considering the amount of time many of us spend on the phone, it is understandable that we sometimes cringe when we hear the phone ring.

Fortunately the method used to redirect energies when talking directly with people can also be used over the phone. Anytime a conversation starts to drain you, use the "Talk to the Hand" technique. Or better yet, begin the technique before all conversations.

When you hear the phone ring, use the quick version: Move your focus from head to heart, be like the Buddha and say, "Trust-flow" from your heart. Next, redirect the energy of whoever you are talking with, allowing them to "talk to the hand." (Speaker phones also work well in a pinch.)

In the words of a busy customer service rep who deals with customers face-to-face and on the phone: "When complaints and accusations start flying, the pen in my hand reminds me to redirect the energy coming at me. Using my hand as a boundary deflects anger and helps me diffuse the situation."

- Boundaries and the Computer -

Invasive energy emanating from a computer can affect the electromagnetic field that surrounds the physical body. An electromagnetic field encircles everyone, playing a large part in keeping the body healthy. (See more about this field in chapter 9.) Taking a few moments to set a neutral boundary before turning on the computer will create a buffer between it's energy and your body. Since this boundary is made up of inner core light and is powered by the energies, you can renew it all day. You will notice the difference in the way your body feels when you take time to set this healthy boundary.

While waiting for your computer to boot up, take a moment to feel the energy of your computer with your hand. How would you describe it? Move your focus from head to heart, and become like the Buddha. Light up your inner core with earth and potential energy by saying, "Trust-flow." Take a deep breath, and as you exhale allow your inner light to surround you, creating a healthy boundary between you and your computer. As the energies flow out your hand, you will feel it create a buffer between the computer's invasive energy and you.

A web database developer explains: "I can spend up to twelve hours at a time writing a custom script with the deadline tick, tick, ticking. If I take a moment to set a boundary, my body responds and I feel like I've caught a second wind."

- Boundaries and Empowerment -

If your job involves supervision, caretaking, counseling, or teaching, you deal with immense responsibility, split-second decision making, a wide range of personalities, and face considerable stress. When situations seem out of hand, you may resort to control as the quickest way to remedy a situation. Control may seem like an easier solution than allowing others to find their own answers with your guidance.

In such circumstances, understanding the difference between healthy and unhealthy energy exchanges can improve communication and help balance a heavy workload. Communication involves much more than just words; body language, tone, and intent also send potent messages to others. The more self-aware you are, the healthier your interactions will be. Although you may be convinced you are empowering others by the words you choose, your energy exchange could be sending another message. For example, you may be allowing people under your supervision to get too close to your personal space, creating an unhealthy pattern of dependency that could result in having to shoulder their burdens. Conversely, expanding too much energy toward people under your supervision can be an invasion of their personal space, making them feel overpowered instead of empowered.

Setting healthy boundaries daily, and knowing when to expand or pull in your energy field, will send a clear message of empowerment instead of a mixed message that confuses everyone involved. Best of all, when your personal space is clear of other's energies, there is more energy for you. With increased energy, you will have more patience to empower others to find their own solutions instead of resorting to control.

A primary school teacher's anecdote: "The amount of energy and decision making involved with teaching a group of children every day is enormous. Using the "Trust-flow" tools allows me to keep up with the pace of my kindergartners. Setting my boundaries in the morning gives me personal space and reaction time. I am then able to let the children work out their problems and find their own solutions, instead of reacting and coping to each situation as it arises."

Teacher with strong boundary

Teacher with weak boundary

Teacher with healthy boundary

Projected Energy Exercise

Allow this exercise to happen, rather than forcing it.

~Ask someone you know to try the following exercise with you, taking turns being the energy sender and receiver.

~Stand facing each other about six feet apart and decide who will be the first energy sender.

~Sender: Close your eyes and move your focus to your mental center. Imagine a shadow or a silhouette of yourself standing in front of you.

~Project this shadow across the room and picture it standing directly in front of the receiver.

~Ask the receiver if they can feel your projected energy. Ask them to describe the feeling. Is it heavy, warm, cool, tingling, or like pressure? Ask them where in their body they feel your energy.

~Pull your energy back by imagining your shadow returning to you.

Observe how it felt projecting your energy. Did your body feel stressed?

~Take turns projecting and retracting energy, paying attention to the different sensations you both feel.

Practicing this exercise will give you an understanding of how you use your energy. If you notice yourself projecting too much energy toward others or pulling in your energy too much, this exercise will help you recognize and change unhealthy energy interactions.

A senior engineer's experience with boundaries. "In the past, certain clients and coworkers would consistently invade my space and by the end of the day their energy would collect in my gut. During the course of Gina's seminar, I realized lots of people unconsciously use their energy to manipulate others. Setting healthy boundaries throughout my day keeps me free of power games and leave me with more energy after work."

Expanding your inner core light around you on a daily basis will transform energy patterns, allowing you to establish healthy boundaries and improve relationships. Remember, you cannot change other people, but you *can* change yourself. Surrounding yourself with a three-foot personal space of inner core light establishes a neutral boundary that you can renew throughout the day. Healing your unhealthy patterns frees you up and invites people who are part of these patterns to respond to you in different ways.

Boundary Exercise

Key phrase: "Head to heart, be the Buddha, trust-flow"
Try this exercise first thing in the morning and throughout the day.
Remember to allow this exercise to happen, rather than forcing it.

~Sit back and close your eyes.

~Allow your focus to move from head to heart and be like the Buddha.

~Imagine the earth sending up a huge hand to support your body throughout the day. Allow this hand to ground your body.

~Now, place your hand at your heart and say, "Trust." Sink into the earth's support.

~Imagine the soles of your feet opening wide and allowing earth energy to flow into your body. Picture the top of your head opening wide and permitting potential energy to flow into your body. Start the flow of energies by saying from your heart, "Flow." These two energies will mix together and light up your inner core.

~Once you feel your inner core light up, take a deep breath. As you exhale, your inner core light will surround your body.

Use your hand as a boundary during conversations and when you are on the phone. Redirect others' energies from your body to your hand and allow them to "Talk to the Hand."

Remember, too, to establish a healthy boundary before using your computer.

Your boundary, or personal space can be replenished all day long by simply saying, "Head to heart, be the Buddha, trust-flow." Then take a deep breath and relax your inner core light around your body.

Chapter Eight

Speakers

Each of us is born with the potential for the unfolding of our true self.
When you deviate from the truth, you are interfering with the
intention of something far greater than you are—
call it nature or a higher power. As a result you develop
discomfort in your body and psyche.
Therefore, anxiety may be regarded as meaningful communication
from a powerful force within you that wants you to be yourself.
—Joyce Ashley

Technology has advanced so rapidly in the last few years that we are truly in an age of information. Computers, cell phones, the Internet, e-mail, and faxes have revolutionized the workplace, making us more productive as a workforce. However, these advances have also placed additional demands on an already busy lifestyle.

Communication available at our fingertips has changed our nine to five workday, enabling us to be accessible morning, noon, and night. Although this development is often financially advantageous, it can take a huge toll on the physical body. Changing from a mental focus to a whole-body awareness is a great way to stay sane and keep up with the demands of today's world.

Understanding the location and function of the seven major energy centers of the body is of special benefit in dealing with added demands. These energy centers—or chakras—are shaped like cones or small speakers, and their main purpose is to send, receive, and process information.

The seven energy centers are constantly imputing and outputting information, expressing who you are and how you are feeling to those around you. At the same time, they absorb and process the information from your immediate environment, helping you make sense of what is happening so you can deal with situations at hand.

If your speakers are healthy and in alignment, they will work together as a whole, giving a clear picture of what is happening. However, if they are bombarded by too much stress or stimulation, you may not be able to understand the input you are receiving. When this happens, your body will send or receive misinformation that can cause all sorts of problems, such as misunderstandings or overreactions to situations.

Our energy centers, or speakers, begin to form when we are babies and are shaped by the many different experiences we have in childhood. Intense experiences can overwhelm the newly forming speakers, causing weak areas in them as we grow. Later, these weak areas may inhibit our ability to cope with life's challenges or to understand ourselves and others. However, in the bigger picture these weak areas bring us lessons to learn.

Acquainting yourself with the energy centers, or speakers, increases your understanding of whole-body awareness. Speakers gives you a road map of your body, so you can pinpoint your weak areas or issues. Learning the location and meaning of each speaker will help you transform attitudes and behaviors that limit you at work and at home.

- 1. The Survival Speaker -

When something as traumatic as losing your home, your job, or your relationship occurs, it can feel like someone just pulled the rug out from under you. This analogy is an accurate way to describe what is happening to you on an energy level in this type of situation. Sudden change that affects your most basic needs can unbalance you, giving rise to feelings of panic and disconnectedness.

The survival speaker is associated with the adrenal gland and is located between the ovaries in women between the ovaries and at the base of the spine in men. This speaker faces downward because it is the main link between your physical body and the earth. If the survival speaker is partially blocked, you may feel uncertain or fearful about the world as a whole. When you do not feel secure and supported, your ability to meet your basic needs can be affected.

Trauma or an unstable upbringing can cause this weak connection in the survival speaker. A weakened connection with the earth may leave you feeling insecure, which in turn can affect your personal life and your performance at work. Quietly sitting outside will allow your survival speaker to reconnect with the earth, thus giving you the support you need to cope with adversity and helping you feel safe and secure.

The survival speaker can also be affected by faulty programming throughout childhood. Up to the age of seven, you are absorbing pertinent survival information from your parents or primary caregivers through this speaker, whether or not the information is accurate. The environment you grow up in and your own connection with the earth also influences early survival programming.

From ages seven to eighteen, you are unconsciously adding your own experiences to the storehouse of information or misinformation that you have absorbed from whomever has raised you. With any awareness of this activity, you would be able to sift through your parents' survival programming, keeping valid information and discarding the rest. Because this process is unconscious, you may one day find yourself running on faulty programming that has nothing to do with who you really are. Such misinformation can create limitations in some areas of your life. Grounding and clearing your survival speaker allows you to own and release old emotions and inaccurate programming so you can attract stability in your life.

You may also need to ground and clear this speaker if you are financially secure but unfulfilled by your career. Connecting your survival speaker with the earth lights up the inner core and puts you in touch with your inner self. Because your inner core contains your deepest desires, connecting with this core will align you with your purpose. You can then attract the most rewarding career while at the same time meeting your needs. Everyone has a right to enjoy a career and find a deeper meaning in the way they make a living.

Taking a few moments to ground and clear your survival speaker can also make a huge difference in the way your workday progresses. Grounding and clearing your survival speaker is best accomplished by sitting outdoors and reconnecting with the earth. Anytime this is not possible, the following technique can help.

If you feel insecure or unsupported during your workday, take a moment to close your eyes and move your focus to the base of your spine. If this area feels tight or tense, place your hand at your heart center and say, "Trust." When you feel the support from the earth, say, "Flow." Earth energy and potential energy will clear your survival speaker, at the same time renewing your connection with the earth and giving you the support you need. Take a deep breath and as you exhale, your inner core light will clear your survival speaker.

- 2. The Emotional Speaker -

With all of the problems in the workplace involving displaced emotions and sexual harassment, understanding the emotional speaker can be of great benefit. The emotional speaker, located directly below the naval and associated with the gonad gland, is where you express your feelings and respond emotionally to others. For example, any emotional or sexual attraction you feel for another person comes from this center. Because this speaker is inputting and outputting intense as emotions, it is easily overwhelmed, causing confusion about whose feelings are whose.

The emotional speaker has a front and back to it. The front of the speaker is where you express your feelings and emotions and also receive emotional input from others. If you are led by your emotions, the front of this speaker will be enlarged, whereas if you avoid emotional exchanges, the front of the speaker might be weak or partially closed. The back of the speaker involves emotional support issues. Do you emotionally support yourself or do you rely on others for emotional support?

Grounding and clearing the emotional speaker allows you to own and release old emotions and also become more aware of what you are transmitting to the world on an emotional level. Setting healthy boundaries in this energy center will improve emotional patterns with others.

A quick check of your emotional speaker in the morning or during your day can prevent unhealthy exchanges before they start. Take a moment to close your eyes and move your focus to your stomach. If this area feels tight or tense, place your hand on your emotional speaker and say, "Trust." When you feel the support from the earth, say, "Flow." Take a deep breath, and as you exhale, earth energy and potential energy will light up your inner core and clear your emotional speaker.

- 3. The Power Speaker -

Power games are commonplace in today's corporate world. The first step in finding a solution to this type of conflict is knowing where in your body the interaction is taking place. The next step is disengaging from it by setting healthy boundaries. Keep in mind that you cannot change the energy patterns of others, but you can change your own.

The power speaker, located in the middle of the torso and associated with the pancreas gland, involves the will and personal power. Whether you are the sender or receiver in a power trip, becoming aware of how you use your energy *can* change your role as either aggressor or victim.

Like the emotional speaker, the power speaker has both a front and a back. If you rely on your will to control others, the front of the power speaker will be enlarged, whereas if you subordinate your will to the desires of others, it may be weak or contracted. If the back of your power speaker is weak or partially closed, you will not feel powerful in your own right and may, as a result, misuse your power in an attempt to control others.

If your stomach is in knots most of the time or you notice others clutching their stomach when they are around you, it is time to ground and clear your power speaker. When you are se-cure in who you are, you can use your personal power wisely in daily interactions, empowering others instead of engaging in petty power trips. By setting a neutral boundary with your inner core light, you can change your role in such games, whether you are the victim or the aggressor.

If you find yourself in a power struggle during your day, move your hand to the middle of your torso and say to yourself, "Trust-flow." Take a deep breath, and as you exhale, your inner core light will clear your speaker while disengaging you from the conflict.

- 4. The Heart Speaker -

The phrase "come from your heart" might not seem to fit in today's aggressive and competitive work setting, but it can work effectively and ethically for everyone, in even the most challenging encounters. The heart speaker is where your personal truth resides, and is a neutral place where you can speak and be heard any time communication is breaking down.

Located in the center of the chest and associated with the thymus gland, this energy center is where you express and receive love, where your personal truth and compassion resides. Although these traits may not be seen much in today's workplace, they are nonetheless much needed.

The heart speaker has a front and a back like the emotional and power speakers. When there are blocks in the front of this speaker, the person may have a hard time expressing their personal truth, compassion, or love. If the back of the heart speaker is blocked, the person may attract painful experiences or feel victimized by others.

Since the heart speaker is where you express your personal truth, it is critical to keep this energy center balanced and clear. In a situation where it is important to be heard and comprehended, speaking from your heart allows you to be understood by everyone.

Grounding and clearing the heart speaker on a regular basis will help process emotions. It will also enable you to release old hurts that keep you from growing.

A quick check of your heart speaker in the morning or during your day can prevent unhealthy exchanges before they start. Take a moment to close your eyes and move your focus to your heart. If your speaker feels tight or tense, place your hand on it and say, "Trust." When you feel the support from the earth, say, "Flow," allowing earth energy and potential energy to clear it. Take a deep breath, and as you exhale, your inner core light will shine through the speaker and set a boundary.

- 5. The Communication Speaker -

Communication has an increasingly important role in today's workplace. Arriving at work, you check your e-mail, voice-mail, and make and return calls. Because much of your interaction with others is not face-to-face, selecting your words carefully is of vital importance. The old adage "Actions speak louder than words" may not apply in many future situations because you may not *see* people during interactions.

The communication speaker, located in the throat and associated with the thyroid gland, involves communication of all sorts including speaking, listening, writing, drawing, or playing music. In addition to all these forms of communication, this speaker also entails honesty with yourself and others.

The communication speaker has a front and back, as do other centers. The front of this speaker deals with how you communicate with others. If the front of your communication speaker is enlarged, you may interrupt others, not allowing them to finish sentences. If you do not express your point of view and agree with others much of the time, the front of your communication speaker may be weak or contracted. The back of the emotional speaker is about listening and honesty. Are you a good listener? Do you tend to gossip? Are your dealings with others misleading or dishonest?

Grounding and clearing the communication speaker helps resolve any misunderstandings, allowing you to express yourself clearly. At the same time it helps enhance all aspects of your work in a competitive world.

- 6. The Mental Speaker -

Because a common occurrence in today's society is to keep our focus in the mind, the mental speaker is especially overtaxed in our busy world. Located in the middle of the forehead and associated with the pituitary gland, this speaker involves the ability to focus, and houses imagination, insight, and intuition.

The front of the mental speaker contains the imagination, ideas, goals, and vision, while the back is engaged with attention to details and the ability to implement ideas and goals. If you know where you want to go in life, but are not able to put your vision and ideas into practice, your mental speaker a clear front and a blocked back. If you attend to all the details in your life but don't have any idea where you want to go or how to reach major goals, the back of your speaker is in good shape but the front may have blocks or weak areas.

Grounding and clearing the mental speaker will help with headaches, focus, and attention span problems. When you take care of this speaker, you will be able to identify your goals in life and know how to reach them.

- 7. The Crown Speaker -

Have you ever wondered if there is more to life than surviving the weekdays and looking forward to weekends and vacation? Since most of our time is spent at work, our job should be rewarding and fulfilling. A clear crown speaker can put us in touch with our purpose and aid us in this endeavor. The crown speaker, located on the top of the head and associated with the pineal gland, involves goals, purpose, potential, wisdom, inspiration, vision and spiritual beliefs.

The crown speaker faces the universe and connects you with your higher goals and potential. If you were brought up with strict beliefs, a need for control, or lots of guilt, you probably have some weak areas or blocks in this speaker. Similarly, if you have put all your efforts into reaching your goals and then find them unfulfilling, you may have a defective crown speaker.

Just as the survival speaker supplies you with a feeling of belonging, the crown speaker enables you to feel a part of the universe. You must have strong connections with both speakers to feel truly secure in who you are. Grounding and clearing your crown speaker will provide you with the inspiration you need to reach goals and achieve your highest potential.

A quick check of your crown speaker first thing in the morning and intermittently throughout the day will help you feel clear-headed. Take a moment to close your eyes and move your focus to the top of our head. If this area feels tight or tense, place your hand on it and say, "Trust." When you feel support from the earth, say, "Flow." Earth energy and potential energy will clear the speaker. Take a deep breath and as you exhale, inner core light will shine through the speaker and connect you with your highest potential.

A chiropractor has this to say about the value of speaker awareness: "I know that healing involves body, mind, and spirit. In case after case, the correlation of emotions to physical symptoms is very apparent. Throughout the day, my knowledge of the speakers and my intuition work together, spurring me on to ask my patients the right questions that will lead to their healing solution."

Speaker Exercise

Key phrase: "Head to heart, be the Buddha, trust-flow"

~Close your eyes and be like the Buddha, allowing everything to flow to you.

~Move your focus around your body. If one of your speakers feels tight or tense, try the following:

> ~Place your hand on your speaker and say from that spot, "Trust."

> ~When you feel the support from the earth, say "Flow." The energies will allow you to own old emotions and clear your speaker.

> ~Take a deep breath and as you exhale, your inner core light will shine through the speaker and set a boundary. Renew this boundary during the day if needed.

Crown Speaker

Mental Speaker

Communication Speaker

Heart Speaker

Power Speaker

Emotional Speaker

Survival Speaker

Note: Later in the day while relaxing, place your hand on the speaker and say, "Trust-flow." Your hand will attract and neutralize any energy stuck within the speaker, transforming it into fluid and flowing energy. Your inner core light and the energies will ground and balance your speaker.

Chapter Nine

Personal Space

So sometimes all our identities become pushed into the background
as we take in bad energy or maybe as we, I don't know,
grow up and get a job or something...
—Ani Difranco

As we approach the millennium, the world is becoming more complex and crowded. Every day, we are constantly surrounded with the hustle and bustle of people, traffic, noise, and deadlines.

Finding ways to cope with so much outer stimuli is essential for your well-being. One way to do this is by creating a healthy personal space around you. Your personal space then acts as a buffer zone between your body and the busy world you live in. Grounding and clearing your personal space will give you reaction time in tense or important meetings, as well as other interactions.

This space already exists, and is known as your energy field or aura; it expresses who you are and what you are feeling at any given moment. Whether or not it is healthy is another matter. A healthy energy field is made up of three feet of personal space that can be divided into five levels. Comprehending each of these levels will increase your awareness and help you understand yourself and others.

- 1. The Physical Level -
Energy contained within the body makes up the physical level. If you are active and in touch with your body, the energy within it will feel light and fluid. If there is an area that harbors a traumatic experience, is in pain,

or causes you discomfort, this area will become dense and heavy. You may gain weight in these areas and unconsciously disown this part of yourself. An area that has held blocked energy for a prolonged time will separate from the energy flow of the body and create disease.

For example, during my first year of kayaking, I hit my face on some rocks in shallow water—an experience that made me more aware of responses in my body. While the cuts and bruises on my face healed immediately, the fear I felt every time I rolled underwater made me realize I had more to heal than just my physical body. To overcome my fears, I used the "Trust-Flow" method every time I felt the fear resurface. Each time I did this, the fear diminished until eventually I was able to feel safe underwater again.

To reclaim an area of the body that is in pain, has been traumatized, has gained weight or feels disowned, lay your hand on the area and say from your heart, "Trust-flow." Allow the stuck energy from the area to flow into your hand. Imagine your hand neutralizing and transforming the blocked energy into fluid energy. It is also helpful to gently rub an area that is dense or blocked, otherwise it tends to be neglected. You and your body can then function again harmoniously.

- 2. The Etheric Level -

The level closest to the physical body is called the etheric level. Derived from the word *ether*, meaning the state between energy and matter, this level consists of the magnetic field or netlike covering that surrounds the physical body, extending one to two inches beyond it. This level acts as a buffer or boundary between the physical body and the next layer, the emotional level. The etheric level can become damaged or weak when we experience trauma in our lives. Smoking, drinking, and drugs also greatly affect the etheric level's ability to separate the

Etheric Level

physical body from the emotional and mental levels, and can adversely affect health. When someone is missing a limb or another part of their body, the etheric level still holds the basic shape of the missing part, which may explain why people still feel sensations associated with missing body parts.

When this healthy barrier is weakened, the emotional level can press on the physical body and cause you to feel depressed. Although antidepressants can provide a temporary relief, they create an artificial barrier between the emotional level and the physical body, and may weaken the etheric level, separating you from your emotions. Remember, emotions are the psyche's way of saying "That's enough" when your mental part might still find ways to cope. Moreover, if the emotional level impinges on your physical body, the resulting stress can cause numerous physical problems. Grounding and clearing the etheric level on a regular basis will strengthen it and improve coping skills.

- 3. The Emotional Level -

The emotional level is where the emotional baggage that people talk about is stored. How you are feeling and how much you have or have not dealt with your emotions radiates in this ever-changing level. This level extends eight to ten inches beyond the etheric level depending on how full it is. If you feel depressed much of the time, it could be that your emotional level is full and is pressing against the etheric level, creating a feeling of depression. You need to empty this level on a regular basis as you would an overflowing vacuum bag or garbage can. Clearing this part of your personal space can make a big difference in the way you operate and feel.

Emotional Level

If you are predominantly a logical thinker, you still need to be aware of your emotional level. Avoidance of your emotions only works for so long and can eventually lead to a breakdown. On the other hand, if you process predominantly through feelings, you will tend to bring more emotions into your space than would a logical thinker, and will fill up your emotional level more quickly.

The best solution to such a situation is to work within both the emotional and mental levels to create a healthy balance. Grounding and clearing these levels daily every morning will give you a clean slate to start your day. If during the day your personal space becomes cluttered with your emotional and mental processing as well as the stress and emotions of others, you can ground and clear your levels again. This simple exercise can make a huge difference in the way you feel and the burdens you carry around.

- 4. The Mental Level -

The mental level, the next layer out in your personal space, involves logic, linear thinking, and mental expression. This level extends eight to ten inches beyond the emotional level. It can fill up and press against the emotional level and physical body, affecting mental health.

When your thoughts are racing out of control, taking a few moments to ground and clear this level can bring instant relief. Since too much mental strain can cause headaches and insomnia, try moving your focus from head to heart to alleviate or prevent these ailments, giving the mental level a much needed break. Clearing this level on a daily basis will positively affect your mental health. With a clear mental level, you can focus on what is most important on your day's agenda and express your ideas in an organized manner.

Mental Level

- 5. The Astral Level -

The astral level is the fifth layer surrounding your body. It extends one to one and a half feet beyond the mental level. This level contains your subconscious parts and projects and magnifies any repressed emotions you may not be aware of. This is also the level where you connect with your dreams.

This level is wild, untamed, and does not respond well to control. It can create problems when you least expect them. For example, just when you think you know who you are and where you want to go in life, some subconscious part of you may step in and wreak havoc with your plans. However, grounding and clearing this level will neutralize any emotions or patterns that are likely to sabotage your goals or happiness. When this level is clear, you can project a lucid reflection of who you are to the world. Moreover, clearing the astral level before sleep will help you remember dreams and allow you to make an easier transition to wakefulness with more clarity.

Astral Level

You can clear all five levels in a standing or sitting position. First, raise your hands over your head, moving them in an arc to bring them down to your sides. This is the movement you will use for the following exercise. In the preceding chapters, you initiated a trust with your inner core. The next step is to let go and allow the inner core to clear your levels without your conscious help. Letting go is something everyone needs to practice, and learning to trust your inner core is a good way to start.

Move your focus from head to heart and raise your hands above your head. Connect with your inner core by saying from your heart, "Trust-flow." Keep your focus at your heart and allow your hands to be guided down to your sides by your inner core. Your arms will start to move seemingly by themselves, making an arc and attracting any blocked etheric, emotional, mental, or astral energy in your personal space. If your arms begin to feel heavy as they move downward, consider it a good sign. When your hands reach your sides, shake your arms to remove any energy that is clinging to them. If your personal space still feels heavy, repeat the following exercise.

Learning to let go and allow your inner core to take over might require a little practice. Remember to relax, and experience, your clear part will show you how to let go.

If there is limited time or space, do the same steps without the arm movement: shift your focus from head to heart, be like the Buddha, and light up your personal space by saying from your heart, "Trust-flow." Take a deep breath, and as you exhale, your inner core light will neutralize the blocked energy in your personal space and send it into the earth.

Clear your personal space the first thing in the morning, as needed throughout the day, and before bedtime. You will feel the difference in the way you carry yourself and how others respond to you.

An executive recruiter has this to say about clearing her personal space: "My job can be extremely demanding and stressful. Since I am paid on a straight commission basis, the constant pressure to produce can be a heavy load to carry. Some mornings in the past, it took everything I had just to enter my office. Clearing my levels throughout the day renews me mentally and emotionally. No matter who I have just talked with, I can take a moment to clear my space from the conversation, reclaim my center, and become my true self again."

In the words of a front office receptionist: "I am the first friendly face people see as they walk through the door. The job's expectations are to stay as attentive and upbeat as possible throughout the day. The constant bombardment of answering phones and greeting the public is mentally and emotionally wearing. When I feel I am at my wit's end, I clear both my personal space and my work space, immediately feeling the change in myself and in the office."

Personal Space Exercise

Key phrase: "Head to heart, be the Buddha, trust-flow"
Remember to allow the exercise to happen, rather than forcing it.
Relax—everything will flow to you.

~Move your focus from head to heart and be like the Buddha.

~Raise your hands over your head. Light up your personal space and connect with your inner core by saying from your heart, "Trust-flow."

~Keep your focus on your heart and allow your arms to be guided by your inner core. Your arms will start to move on their own and will attract and collect any stuck emotions or mental energy within your space. If your arms feel weighted down as they move toward your body, consider this a good sign.

~When your hands reach your sides, take a moment to shake your arms and remove any stuck energy still clinging to them. If your personal space is feeling very heavy, repeat this exercise.

~If there is limited time or space, you can do the same steps without the arm movement.

Clear your personal space first thing in the morning, as needed throughout your busy day, and before you go to bed at night. You will feel the difference in the way you carry yourself and how others respond to you.

Chapter Ten

Intuition

Wise people have an inward sense of what is beautiful,
and the highest wisdom is to trust the intuition and be guided by it.
—Aristotle

We are living in an age of immediate information, instant gratification, and constant transition. Keeping up with the new advances in science, the economy, and world affairs can sometimes leave us exhausted and disillusioned. In our fast-paced world the old securities we relied on in the past—family, home, and jobs—are also changing, challenging us to find security within ourselves.

There is the potential inside us to know who we are and what our deepest desires are. This potential resides in our inner core, and has the ability to answer our deepest questions and to access information unavailable to our outer senses. It offers us a new way of communicating with ourselves—in a sense, a new intelligence. The "knowingness" that arises combines information from the conscious and subconscious minds, logic, feelings, and most of all, intuition. Communicating with our inner core can, and should, happen throughout a busy workday.

Animals, children, and cultures in touch with the earth's rhythms rely on instincts and inner senses more than people caught up in the frenzied pace of today's workplace. When we are young, we are in touch with these inner senses, but as we grow up we are taught to depend more on our outer senses. Later, as we enter the adult world, our subtle inner perceptions may be dismissed as nonsense or ignored.

However, utilizing both inner and outer senses consciously during the workday will heighten your awareness of your surroundings and the people you work with. This combination will also enhance your creativity, help you find new ways to juggle your busy schedule, and improve your people skills and problem-solving abilities. Using your knowingness consciously throughout the day will ultimately increase your productivity in the work-place.

Actually, although five outer senses guide you in everyday life, you are also using your inner senses. You may not be aware of these senses, perhaps simply calling their signals a hunch, an insight, a flash of intuition or imagination. Regardless of what you call them, the key is to start paying attention to them. Changing your focus from head to heart and lighting your inner core with the energies will make you more conscious of these senses and give you an added edge. As a result, your workday will feel more sane and your outlook will expand and improve.

Most of us have experienced a time when we were in touch with our intuition. A strong feeling, a gut reaction, took hold deep within us, and we knew just how to act or when to take a chance. This knowingness tends to arise in times of crisis, or when we are at a crossroads in life. But why wait for a crisis to experience intuition?

When first attempting to consciously use intuition, you might perceive it to be a mental struggle, something that will take lots of hard work to accomplish. Much of that struggle comes from staying in the mind, trying to control your thoughts so that you can hear your inner information. Moving your focus from head to heart can solve this dilemma. Your heart speaker holds your personal truth and is an ideal place to start to communicate with your intuition and inner self. When you focus in your heart, there is no need to worry about quieting your thoughts. Your inner information will flow to you because you are sitting in your calm center like the Buddha. Everything, even knowingness, flows to the Buddha.

Learning this new way of accessing your intuition takes some practice and trust. To succeed you will need patience and a willingness to be un-concerned about whether the information you receive is "wrong" or "right." Tapping into your knowingness is like learning a new language. Each step of the way it is necessary to learn to ask questions and interpret the answers you receive. However, despite the challenges, this new relationship is one of the most important you can make, for it involves a conscious decision to connect with the clear, knowing part of your psyche.

Intuition uses a multidimensional language similar to that of a dream state, in which feelings, senses, thoughts and pictures blend to create a rich, vivid tapestry that may be interpreted in a variety of ways. Intuition can also present itself as a single thought, feeling, sensory awareness, whisper, or picture.

Potential speaker

Wiring your intuition directly to you establishes a circuitry that can help you access your knowingness on a daily basis. For this you will need to utilize two speakers—an earth speaker, located two feet below you, and a potential speaker, located two feet above your head. Think of your earth speaker as the important link between your physical body and the earth, giving your intuition a solid base or structure. The potential speaker contains pertinent information relating to your higher knowledge, goals, and purpose. Connecting with these two speakers will allow you to access transmissions from your intuition, at the same time giving you a conscious base and receptor.

A simple way to bypass the easily distracted conscious mind is to wire the earth speaker and the potential speaker directly to each of your hands. Once the wiring is in place, all that is needed is to light up the speakers from your inner core and allow your inner core to guide your hands. As you know from the previous chapter, letting your hands be guided by your inner core is a powerful means of letting go. It is also a direct way to tune into your intuition.

Earth speaker

Close your eyes and imagine the speakers above and below you. Light up your inner core and connect with the two speakers by saying from your heart, "Trust-flow." Picture both speakers sending an energy flow to each of your fingers as if through strings on a marionette. Allow your hands to become your inner core's hands, making sure to keep your focus at your heart. When you feel your fingers moving on their own, your hands are ready to receive.

One strategy for registering answers is a two-hand method where you place your hands out in front of you, elbows resting on your lap and palms facing each other about eighteen inches apart. Let one hand represent you and let the other hand represent a prospective job, a client, a relationship, an investment, or whatever it is you want information about. Then, formulate your question as clearly and specifically as possible. If you are imagining yourself in one hand and a new job in the other, you might ask, for example, "Will there be a job opportunity for me in the immediate future?" An even clearer question would be: "Will there be a *more fulfilling* job opportunity for me in the immediate future?"

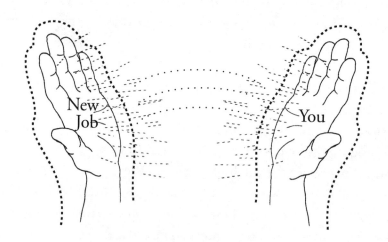

Ask your questions out loud, since outward expression helps start the flow of intuitive information. Then turn the control of your hands over to your inner core. If your hands feel like they are being drawn together in a steady flowing motion, this is a positive sign meaning there will be promising opportunities coming your way. If your hands do not move, or start to move and then stop, this might mean there are no opportunities in the immediate future, or if there are, they could entail delays or setbacks.

Your next question might be: "Does this mean I need to focus on my present job and learn something more there?" Your intuition will feed you each new question while teaching you its own unique language.

Another strategy for registering answers with your hands is a yes-no method similar to kinesiology, or muscle testing. For this approach you can either consciously set up finger or hand movements for yes and no, or simply allow your inner core to assign the movements. Some examples my clients have used in the past are a thumb up for yes, a thumb down for no; one hand opening up for yes, the hand closing for no; as well as a tingling sensation in a finger or hand for yes, and no sensation for no.

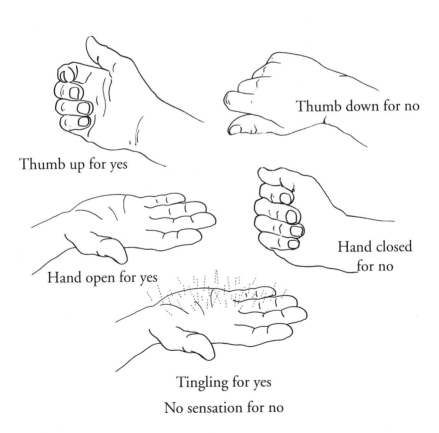

Thumb down for no

Thumb up for yes

Hand closed for no

Hand open for yes

Tingling for yes

No sensation for no

Letting your inner core assign the movements will create an immediate bond of trust with your intuition. If this seems difficult at first, then you might feel more comfortable consciously establishing your finger or hand movements. Once you have a clear code for yes and no, you are ready to test your intuition. Do this by asking at least three sample questions, one at a time, that you already know the answers to such as, "Are my eye's blue?" "Do I have two children?" "Am I five foot six inches tall?" Remember to ask your questions out loud when possible, then wait patiently for your intuition to respond with a finger or hand movement. If an answer is incorrect, don't worry; simply shift your focus to your heart, then say "Trust-flow," wait a moment, and try again. Approach this exercise with playfulness, imagination, and spontaneity, since with inner exerciss of this sort allowing works better than trying.

Now think of some questions you have been waiting to ask and phrase them clearly and concisely, formatting them to yes-no responses. While waiting for an answer, pay attention to any thought, feeling, sensory awareness, or picture that comes to you, and know this is your intuition communicating. Even though you are working with a method, your inner core will always give you more than you ask for. If you are asking about money, for instance, and you see the color green but you get the feeling it is far away, ask out loud if this means there is money coming but not immediately. Then if your fingers register a yes, consider budgeting your money for a while.

Yes-no's are also great ways for verifying intuitive information you receive during the day. If you feel apprehensive while leaving your office, for instance, you might ask your intuition if this is something worth paying attention to. With practice, you may soon find your yes-no's coming to the rescue instinctively.

One day while waiting for my six-year-old daughter at our neighborhood bus stop, I panicked when the school bus pulled up, emptied out, and she wasn't on it. I immediately asked my inner core if she was okay. And before I could mentally think of an answer, my finger responded with a yes. Intuitively aware that she was safe, I was able to calm down enough to retrace her steps and discover she had gotten off the bus at a friend's house. That was the day my trust in my intuition could no longer be challenged.

"An engineer and co-founder of a biochemical firm explains: "I am involved in numerous presentations and tend to be very mental Sometimes during group interactions my ego gets in the way. Taking the time to ground, center, and come from my heart keeps my ego in check and allows my intuitive part to take over. I am then able to read the group more effectively, understand their needs, and reach them in a more balanced and successful manner."

A tutor in a variety of subject areas states: "When a parent asks me for some ideas to help their child and I come up with a plan, my hand will automatically respond with a yes or no signal, and I am able to tell if I am on the right track with the student."

Believing in your intuition will enhance your life and allow you to know yourself on a deeper, more meaningful level. The following exercise will help you access your intuition during the day, while giving it a practical forum in which to express itself.

Intuition Exercise

Key phrase: "Head to heart, be the Buddha, trust-flow"
Remember to allow this exercise to happen, rather than forcing it.
When you sit back and relax; your knowingness will flow to you.

~Close your eyes and move your focus from head to heart.

~Sit like the Buddha in your calm center, allowing your information to flow to you.

~Light up your inner core and connect with your earth and potential speakers by saying from your heart, "Trust-flow." Take a deep breath and as you exhale, your inner core light will surround you.

~Imagine both speakers sending transmissions and attaching to each of your fingers similar to marionette strings. Let your hands become your inner core's hands. When you feel your fingers moving on their own, you are ready.

~Ask your inner core to show you a finger or hand movement for yes by saying, "Trust-flow." Next, ask for a signal for no by saying, "Trust-flow." Test your intuition by asking three sample questions you already know the answers to such as, "Are my eyes blue?" If an answer is incorrect, simply shift your focus to your heart, then say, "Trust-flow." Wait a moment, and try again.

~Ask clear, concise questions using the two-hand method or yes-no method. If you are presented with a picture, a feeling, a sense, or a thought, ask what it means by stating your questions in a yes-no format. Practice frequently, being careful not to judge the information you receive at first. With practice, you will be able to tell the difference between information that has come directly from your intuition and information that has been influenced by your conscious mind.

Conclusion

You have to leave the city of your comfort and go into the wilderness of your intuition. What you'll discover will be wonderful. What you'll discover will be yourself.

—Alan Alda

All of us possess untapped intuitive abilities just waiting to be discovered. Connecting with my intuition was the most important discovery of my life. Growing up, I would often blend with other people's emotions and energy, which left me feeling emotionally drained. Becoming aware of my own intuition has helped me change unhealthy patterns and has allowed me to grow faster than I ever felt possible.

The favorite part of teaching my COREporate Potential Seminars is watching other people start to consciously use and trust their intuition. Even though life is fast-paced and most of us do not have much downtime during our busy days, when we do take a few moments to expand awareness, our inner core and intuition does the rest.

In summary, remember to change your focus from a mental outlook to a whole-body awareness. This shift will allow you to see your world through a broader vision, with a fresh outlook and new insight.

Reconnect with the flow of life by choosing the path of strength. Strength helps you slow down and balance your will, allowing life to lead the way.

Find and enter your calm center and be like the Buddha, setting your goals and intentions from within to attract what you need.

Make sure to enlist the support of the earth and take care of your body by utilizing two free energies: earth energy and potential energy.

Set healthy boundaries with your inner core light while transforming yourself and others with your highest potential.

Keep your speakers and levels clear, so you can transform unhealthy patterns, understand yourself, and be understood by others.

Last and most important, tap into your intuition, so you can use your knowingness throughout your day, align with your purpose, and work within life's balance.

Change is happening more quickly than ever before. Adaptability and insight are the survival skills needed most in the corporate world. Using all inner as well as outer resources available will give you the ability to face the challenges of the future. Taking a few moments in the morning to light up your inner core and access your intuition will give you the adaptability and inner security you need.

Intuition is a special talent we all possess that should be exercised wisely and often. We need to go beyond what the world says is possible and start using *all* our senses. Only then can we meet the challenges of this new millennium.

Glossary

Aura: A luminous radiation that emanates from all living matter; a distinctive atmosphere surrounding a given source.

Awareness: The ability to recognize, understand, and transform what is happening around us.

Chakras: Energy centers within the body, the spinning of which generates an electromagnetic field around the body.

Earth energy: A warm, calming energy that originates at the core of the earth.

Electromagnetic field: An area marked by electromagnetic currents that emanates from all matter.

Etheric level: a netlike layer that surrounds the physical body extending one to two inches beyond it. This level acts as a buffer or boundary between the physical body and the emotional level.

Focus: A position in which something must be placed for clarity of perception.

Grounding: Renewing the connection with the physical body and the earth.

Insight: The power or act of seeing into a situation.

Intention: What one hopes to do or bring about.

Intuition: The power or faculty of obtaining direct knowledge or cognition without evident rational thought or inference.

Kinesiology: Study of the principles of mechanics and anatomy in relation to human movement; also known as muscle testing.

Levels: Different locations and functions of the aura.

Mental focus: A mind focus, predominantly using a thought-based or logical approach.

Personal space: A three-foot area surrounding the body.

Potential energy: A light, airy energy that comes from the universe.

Speaker: An energy center located in or around the body.

Speaker imbalance: A restricted energy flow in an energy center.

Strength: An aptitude for letting go, adapting, and flowing with life.

Will: A faculty used to control life and meet with numerous demands, often at the expense of our well-being.

Whole-body awareness: Paying attention to and using the entire body to process and interpret outer stimuli.

About the Author

Gina Giacomini has been teaching Inner Awareness Seminars to individuals, groups and businesses for the last twelve years. Her background is in teaching and outdoor adventure tours. She has two children and lives in Coloma, California.

Joanne McCubrey

For information on COREporate Potential Seminars:
E-mail: potential@cwo.com
Website: www.whitewater/rafting.net/potential

Order Form

Quantity	Item	Amount
_____	Bringing Intuition to Work ($14.95)	_____
	Sales tax of 7.25% for California residents	_____
	Shipping and handling (see chart below)	_____
	Total amount enclosed	_____

Quantity discounts available

Shipping and handling

	Surface	First Class	Each Additional Book
United States	$3.50	$.50	$.25
Canada	$5.00	$1.00	$.50

Method of Payment

☐ Check or money order enclosed
(make payable to Innervisions Publications, in U.S. currency only)

☐ MasterCard   ☐ Visa

_____   _____
Card Number   Expiration date

Please photocopy this order form, fill it out, and mail it together with your name, address, personal check or money order, or charge card information, to:

INNERVISIONS
PUBLICATIONS
P. O. Box 213
Coloma, CA 95613
E-mail: potential@cwo.com
Website: www.whitewater/rafting.net/potential